Abiding in Identity

Who I Am Because of Whose I Am

Nate Sweeney

Sermon To Book
www.sermontobook.com

Abiding in Identity / Nate Sweeney
ISBN-13: 978-1-945793-61-5
ISBN-10: 1-945793-61-9

One of the hardest parts about discipleship is watching the process of biblical brokenness unfold in people's lives. Jesus taught us that the Kingdom of God is available to all, but it must come through brokenness that leads to repentance (2 Corinthians 7:10). People who recognize their brokenness will, most of the time and eventually, open their hearts to Christ's redemption and forgiveness. This process can be long and brutal, but it is the only way. Being in people's lives during this process can be brutal, too, but that is discipleship.

One of the most joyous parts of discipleship is watching broken people repent of their sins and find forgiveness, love, hope, and joy in Christ. For me, this has been especially moving when I have been with these people as they journey. I have witnessed the transformation unfold.

The joy of watching Christ make beautiful things out of us is priceless. If you are not in messy discipleship ministry, you are missing out on countless hours of painful journey with people. But you are also missing out on joyful bliss when they finally surrender their hearts to Christ. The pain of the journey is not more than the joy of the destination.

Thank You, Jesus, that I get to be part of what You are doing in the earth today in the lives of people. Thank You for taking our ashes and making beauty. Thank You for forgiving me when I have complained about the pain of messy ministry. Thank You for not taking me out of the process, because I have been able to watch Your redeeming hand time and again. You, O God, are simply amazing!

This book is dedicated to you disciples of Christ who call Him Lord. This book is for all of you who are brave enough to live in messy discipleship and minister out of that place of authenticity and transparency. This book is for those of you who have journeyed with people on their road to brokenness. This book is dedicated to all of you who would dare to trust Christ with your entire life. Nothing says, "Lord, I'm Yours" like showing that nothing belongs to you. Thank You for giving selflessly to the Lord first and then to His kingdom.

CONTENTS

Why This Book?... 3

What Is Righteousness?.. 17

Are We Preaching Only Half of the Gospel?.......... 29

Identity Without Christ Versus Identity in Christ 61

Which Covenant Are You Living Under?............... 85

Isn't the Heart Evil? 111

Renew Your Mind.. 129

I Am the Righteousness of God in Christ............. 159

A Tale of Three Kingdoms.................................. 185

Living in Holiness 217

Abiding in Identity— at the Feet of Jesus............ 247

Journaling 101 by Rocky Fleming...................... 265

Further Resources.. 269

Notes.. 273

About the Author... 279

About Sermon To Book 281

Why This Book?

The church is not made up of natural "friends." It is made up of natural enemies. Christians come together, not because they form a natural collocation, but because they have been saved by Jesus Christ and owe him a common allegiance. In the light of this common allegiance, in light of the fact that they have all been loved by Jesus himself, they commit themselves to doing what he says—and he commands them to love one another.[1]

—**D.A. Carson**

I grew up in a religious environment. The church my family was a part of all my childhood had many theological influences that were grounded in truth but that lived in an unbalanced extreme of many of those truths. My experience in this church environment led me to an unhealthy understanding of God.

I left this environment with many confusing theological conclusions. I eventually went through a season when I hated what I thought was the overall Christian church for many years. I loved God—I just hated what I saw His church had become.

I started a journey that I am still on. I asked God to simply reveal Himself to me and show me truth. I asked for any deception in my life to be exposed by His Holy Spirit and His Word. I eventually ended up spending over a year in John 15, learning what it meant to abide in Christ. This simple revelation has transformed my life in ways that religious systems never could. This journey has taken me to many different theological places, and my experiences have led me to important conclusions, one of which is this:

The topic of righteousness with God is the most misunderstood topic in the Christian community today.

That may seem like a pretty bold statement, and it is. Righteousness is the foundation upon which all other theology should be founded. If we do not lay a firm foundation of righteousness, then our walk of faith will falter and maybe even crumble, much like mine did.

I have taught and preached on the topic of righteousness for many years and in many different settings. When it comes to God and who we are in relation to Him, most people I know have a sense of guilt and inferiority. I am not only talking about non-believers; I am talking about Bible-believing Christians.

Nearly every time I speak on righteousness, there are those who pull me aside afterward and want to share inspiring thoughts that came out of the message. Many have shared that they had not seen this view of righteousness in Scripture and they felt the light open up new realms for their relationship with God. Others talked about how this message brought a freedom from religious bondage in which they had felt captive for many years.

Still others have said that they felt the invitation from God to pursue fellowship with Christ and become a disciple of His. Some have bristled at this message and wanted to defend their self-made goodness, arguing that they are good people who live good lives and that this equates into good standing with God. These encouraging and conflicted conversations have led me to believe that this topic of righteousness is misunderstood and that a proper understanding of it is needed in the Body of Christ today.

We Have a Problem

Within humanity there is a sin problem. We are all born with the seed of sin in our nature. This has humanity on a search for righteousness and self-justification. Many religions, humanitarian organizations, charitable foundations, and philanthropic institutions have been created in a search for an answer to this sin problem.

Most people try to do good and try not to do bad in hopes that this will balance out the scales of karma or please a god, any god. I believe most churches are filled with people who are simply doing their Christian duty in hopes that their attendance, donations, and service to the church is enough to appease God and eradicate the sin problem in their lives. But this sin problem is something that is not reconcilable without intervention from God.

In the American Christian church, I see people searching in similar yet different ways. We have many tribes, camps, denominations, sects, and divisions represented. All have their core beliefs, cultural practices, and philosophies of ministry.

I love the diversity in the Body of Christ; however, diversity should not equal division. I see more divisions than I do unity. I see many allowing the few things we disagree on to break down the relationships that are founded on the things we do agree on. This breaks my heart, and I believe it also breaks the heart of God. God is amazing at bringing unity in our diversity, if we will let Him.

Staying United Despite Diversity

Many times, instead of uniting behind what we have in common, we allow the secondary issues to divide us. I have seen the words *apostasy*, *heresy*, *wolf*, and *false teacher* misused more times than I think they were ever properly used in the entire New Testament. As much as some hyper extremes see a demon or angel behind every tree, many on the opposite extreme see heretics and wolves behind every pulpit.

> Some of today's self-appointed heresy hunters are like a doctor who amputated his patient's head because the patient needed eye-glasses. They are like the hypocrites Jesus spoke of who strained out a gnat yet swallowed a camel, damning some of God's children to hell because of a difference over a non-essential doctrine or practice.[2]
> —**Dr. Michael Brown**

I don't deny the validity of apostates, heretics, wolves, and false teachers, but they are not as prevalent as many would purport. Disagreeing on some biblical issues or forms of ministry does not make one a heretic and the other a saint. It's as if some people think that if you and I don't completely agree on everything, then we are enemies and are at war. It should not be this way. I would consider myself a "doctrine nerd"; I adhere closely to a conservative interpretation of Scripture. I am not for a second endorsing those who would seek to deceive others using the Bible. I am simply disappointed by the immaturity I see from many in leadership in the Body of Christ today.

Sometimes I make light about people who use their own religious soapbox and bullhorn to condemn another's religious soapbox and bullhorn. I guess some think that the higher they stand or the louder they yell, the more they will be heard. Tearing down someone else to further your own agenda is not good leadership and is not Christ-like.

I have witnessed many people practicing the same sins of which they are accusing others, all the while emanating an impression of purity in their behavior. They are completely blinded to the hypocrisy in which they are walking. I think some church leaders today are convinced they have a spiritual gift of criticism. Obviously that gift does not exist. If you are hypercritical, you may have a critical spirit, but it's not of the Holy Spirit.

My intention in this book is not to criticize or tear others down, but the opposite. I hope to share biblical insight that will be a catalyst in your life and draw you into a deeper fellowship with Christ. I want to point you to an intimate, abiding relationship with Christ that allows Him to be the transforming agent between you and Himself.

One Extreme or Another

During my many years of experience in the church world, I have seen two common lines of thinking on the topic of righteousness that stand out. These two main ways of thinking both look at the same Bible but come away with completely opposite interpretations of what is meant in the text. The lists ahead offer only a handful of the more extreme views I have come across. They are recorded here as the most common and not an exhaustive listing.

Before I put forth these two lines of thinking, I want to be careful not to paint a bad picture. What I am sharing here is not the mainstream thinking of most Christian groups. I will simply be sharing some characteristics that are fringe and extreme views of two schools of thought I have encountered in my experiences.

These views play a large part in the topic of a right standing with God. There is a huge spectrum of belief on both sides of these two lines of thinking, but through my theology, set forth in the pages of this book, we'll find solace in a balanced view somewhere in the middle.

The first line of thinking:

- Human beings are worms and have no value ever.

- Salvation has nothing to do with me and is done separately from me.

- Even as a Christian, I will never be worthy before God.

- Nothing I do in this life matters, because of God's predetermined choice for my life.

- God's holiness keeps Him distant, and He does not desire a personal relationship with humanity.

The second line of thinking:

- Human beings can attain a godlike status through faith and good works.

- Salvation has everything to do with me, and I am responsible to earn and maintain God's favor through good works.

- My faith and good works can determine my destiny and circumstances. I have ultimate control even outside of a sovereign God.

- God is bound to cooperate with my faith and do things according to my confessions and desires.

- Righteousness is earned by walking in obedience to God's Word.

Looking at the list above, what are you thinking? Are you familiar with either of those lines of thought? Do those statements sit well with you, or do they cause you concern? Do any of these ideas seem extreme or unbalanced?

This Is Your Season of Change!

I am truly amazed at the paths that God has led me down in my life. Many I would not have chosen myself, but I have yielded to His choosing. Many were painful, full of discipline, pruning, and rebuke, but so very fruitful. Many seasons were blessed and prosperous as well as full of pain and sorrow.

In studying the book of Ecclesiastes recently, I was reminded that God's seasons have purpose and significance (Ecclesiastes 3:1–8). One of my greatest life lessons, which has been a constant in all seasons, has been to ask God questions like:

- "What are You doing in this season?"
- "What do You want to teach me?"
- "Where is this leading me?"
- "Who am I learning from and who am I teaching in this season?"

The seasons are not about me, but they always have important lessons for me on this journey of discipleship with Christ.

I am learning that Jesus' words of simplistic, child-like faith should be the approach I take in all situations. I should view the world with endless possibilities in Christ. I should view the world through the awe and splendor of this amazing God. I should look at every mountain as movable and insignificant compared to my God (Matthew 17:20). I should be reminded daily that my God took nothing and created something (Genesis 1). And then He imparted value into that something. This something is me. This something is humanity. This something is this world. I am more than a pawn on the chessboard of life; I am a child of the Highest King, seated in the heavenly places in Christ (Romans 8:12–17; Ephesians 1:15–23).

As we embark on this journey, I encourage you to adopt this mindset. Open yourself up to learning new things about righteousness. Strive to dig deep and seek God. And above all, allow Him to guide you to truth.

Faith at the Center

We are created in God's image and likeness, and He desires fellowship with us. All He asks of us to walk in fellowship with Him is faith: Faith that is identified by personal abandonment and absolute trust. Faith that acts in obedience. Faith that says, "I am not my own, I have been bought with a price" (1 Corinthians 6:19–20).

That price was the precious blood of Christ, and the payment He supplied gave huge significance to my life. He wants me to have faith that takes the call to crucifixion with Christ seriously and lives accordingly.

Faith that knows I have been crucified with Christ and that it is no longer I who live but Christ who lives within me (Galatians 2:20). Faith that knows that I was buried with Him in baptism and raised with Him in new life (Romans 6:4). Faith that understands that I am hidden in Him

(Colossians 3:3). Faith that is determined to live in an intimate, abiding relationship with Him.

It would be dishonoring to God to call insignificant what He has called significant. It would be shameful for me to live my life outside of what He has called me to be and to do.

So, this is where I am today. It's where I was yesterday and where I will be tomorrow. I am in the inner chamber with Christ. I am sitting at His feet. I am longing to hear His voice impart love, worth, grace, mercy, peace, and joy to me. This fellowship is where I live. This fellowship is what compels me to make Christ known to the world. I know Him intimately, and I am compelled to bring this to others.

My heart is to invite you into this conversation as I open the Scriptures and see what God says about the topic of righteousness and our identity. I ask that as you turn the pages ahead, you remove the goggles of your previous theology and ask the Lord to open your eyes to see what the Spirit is revealing to you. Ask the Holy Spirit to speak loudly so that you will clearly hear what He is saying on this topic.

Thank you for taking the time to invest in your spiritual growth through this book.

Workbook Sections with a Journal Prompt

At the end of each chapter in this book, you will find an application-focused workbook section that will help you delve deeper into the material and develop concrete steps to put these abiding principles to work for your individual needs. In each workbook section, there will also be a journal prompt. In Appendix A, you will find the STAR journaling grid, which is designed to help you discover how to journal in a meaningful way.[3]

I want you to understand that journaling is another form of communication with God and can become a lifestyle. This can happen if you feel connected to God through His Word. This connection happens when you read His Word and apply it to your life in the circumstances you are dealing with.

As we move forward in this book, it is important that you understand that the process you will be going through will require that you learn to "self-feed" on God's Word. You can get a journal to accompany this book or use whatever works best for you.

In using the journal, you will experience a process that will help you become a self-feeder. This process will likely continue for the rest of your life. I understand that many people initially feel a little intimidated by journaling, until they come to see that it is not as hard or as complicated as they feared it would be.

The Swoosh

Years ago, in prayer, I had a vision of a day when I would author many books that would help spread the gospel of Christ to the nations. During that vision, I saw what I could only describe as a smeared fingerprint. I knew what it meant immediately. In the environment in which I grew up, we took the biblical model of anointing with oil seriously.

If you have ever taken some oil on your finger and applied it to a doorpost, to someone's forehead, or to a sheet of paper, you know the smeared fingerprint that is left behind. In this vision, I had the understanding that I wanted to anoint each copy of my books, which would leave that smeared look. I wrote this in my journal and left it there.

Years later, as I began to see the dreams of authoring Christ-centered books come to pass, I was reminded of this. Although I cannot personally anoint every book, I decided to use what I call a swoosh to designate that each book has been prayed over. My prayer is that the words in the books published will be anointed by God, bring life transformation to all who read them, and bring glory to God.

About The Abiding Network

The vision of The Abiding Network, of which I am the founder and directional leader, is to assist leaders in creating environments of discipleship to encourage followers to know Christ and make Him known.

Abiding Network was launched out of Catalyst Church in Bentonville, Arkansas, in 2013. This is a support network for church leaders who are active in ministry to know Christ and make Him known in their area of influence.

Our heart is to network individuals, churches, nonprofits, and other groups to support their Kingdom calling. We offer a system of biblical accountability, encouragement, relationship building, and resource sharing to assist in their health and long-term success. As a network, we have partnered with dozens of churches in many diverse areas. Our website (www.abidingnetwork.com) lists some of the organizations and ministries with which we have partnered for Kingdom fruit. As our network grows, we add ministries to our platform so that the network expands as God leads. The intent of Abiding Network members should be to unite in the common vision to know Christ and make Him known. We desire a unity of the Spirit that celebrates what God is doing in our world today.

Coaching

Many leaders in the business and church worlds need an outside voice for encouragement, accountability, leadership development, and organizational strategy. One aspect of The Abiding Network is to serve leaders in such a capacity—for instance, in seasons of building, transition, growth, relationship development, tragedy, and celebration. Some of the most fruitful seasons of our lives can be birthed out of a mentor or coach helping us process through our journey.

We are also developing many leadership resources that are available to help church leaders navigate the short- and long-term direction and vision of their sphere of influence. I personally have been coached, and I myself coach many leaders in many different ministry and secular environments.

I have found coaching to be one of the greatest

catalysts to my personal and professional growth and leadership development. Sometimes we simply need a coach, like Paul was to Timothy, to help us grow into all that God intends for us.

Resources

For more information about The Abiding Network, please visit www.abidingnetwork.com. Media resources can be found at www.abidingnetwork.com/Media.

And please see Appendix B of this book for information about the Journey program and the Influencers ministry, as well as a list of relevant resources—including my books *The Abiding Church* and *Abiding at the Feet of Jesus*, also published by Sermon To Book.

CHAPTER ONE

What Is Righteousness?

What greater rebellion, impiety, or insult to God can there be, than not to believe His promises?[4]

—**Martin Luther**

One of these days some simple soul will pick up the Book of God, read it, *and believe it*. Then the rest of us will be embarrassed.... The fact beats ceaselessly into my brain these days that there is a world of difference between knowing the Word of God and knowing the God of the Word.[5]

—**Leonard Ravenhill**

For He made Him who knew no sin to be sin for us, that we might become the righteousness of God in Him.

—*2 Corinthians 5:21*

Therefore, having been justified by faith, we have peace with God through our Lord Jesus Christ, through whom also we have access by faith into this grace in which we stand, and rejoice in hope of the glory of God.

—Romans 5:1-2

After careful study of the Scriptures, a new believer determined he needed to pursue righteousness. But how to go about this? First, he cleansed his life of any things that caused him temptation. Second, he analyzed his relationships and identified the people in his life whom he believed would benefit his journey through being good examples and the people who could potentially, knowingly or unknowingly, sabotage it. He then made a point to nurture the beneficial relationships while allowing himself to exercise caution with the others. Third, he practiced disciplined routines and habits: he never missed church on Sunday, he volunteered at a local soup kitchen, and he tithed regularly.

A year passed, and he was at a loss. He had certainly cleaned up his life and was living as a remarkable example of Christ. But he didn't feel much closer to God. He had checked all the boxes that he thought would bring him righteousness. What had he missed?

Righteousness Defined

Many people try to interpret the topic of righteousness through a form of preconceived theological leaning or personal interpretation instead of simply seeing what the Bible has to say about it. I would like to undertake an unbiased examination of righteousness and let the Bible define what we are actually talking about.

For years, I sincerely studied and sought out many resources on this topic, because I saw the important role that this would play in my pursuing Christ or walking away from Him. I did not want some preacher or theologian's interpretation to interfere with what God was trying to convey in the biblical texts. After all, righteousness is a hotly discussed topic in many Christian circles. You can find many definitions of what is meant by this word. Defining the term is very important so that we can communicate based on the same understanding.

For the remainder of this book, when I use the word *righteous*, this is what I mean: justified, good, in good standing with God, correct, innocent, upright, morally right.

For the remainder of this book, when I use the word *unrighteous*, this is what I mean: unjust, wrong, evildoer, iniquity, wicked, guilty.

For the remainder of this book, when I use the word *self-righteous*, this is what I mean: justification with God as a direct result of one's own good behaviors, abilities, and avoidance of bad behaviors; one who finds their own way to God.

Righteousness is introduced early in the Bible and is threaded throughout. It really is amazing that it is a common theme that God lays out throughout the Scriptures. It is as if this was God's design from the beginning and He was pursuing this relationship with us even after it was marred in the Garden of Eden.

I think a lot of people have a hard time digesting the revelation that God would, and did, make us righteous. Most Christians live with a sin consciousness even after they are born again. This means that the awareness and thoughts that speak to right standing with God are overshadowed with sin in mind. Many Christians, in my experience, could not or would not confess, "I am the righteousness of God" (2 Corinthians 5:21).

The church has traditionally been good at showing humanity our unrighteousness and our need for a savior. This is a huge part of the gospel message, pre-Christ. However, even after a person is saved, the church tends to teach that our redemption is still on pause until we die and get to heaven.

Promises for Today

Take a look at most of the songs sung and sermons preached in traditional church settings. They look to the hope and promises of the "sweet by and by."[6] They mostly speak to heaven and what it will be like when we attain that part of our salvation. Most of the time you hear that we are barely getting by here on this earth and that we cannot wait to get to heaven.

When I examine Scripture, I see an entirely different story. I see a God who fulfills His promise of redemption now and in eternity. He bestows so many promises on the believer the minute the heart change takes place. He grows us in progressive sanctification and transformation that opens the door to greater revelation of these promises.

As we will see in the pages to come, our salvation opens wide the door to right standing with God now and also in eternity. This lack of understanding on righteousness is why I am taking the time to write this book. What God says about your salvation here and now is enough to transform your life to a place you have never been. The promise of His presence alone is enough to convince anyone of the righteousness provided for them through Christ. Much of the traditional preaching and teaching within the church leans toward humanity still living as slaves to sin and not focusing on the high calling of righteousness. We will look at this more in later chapters, but I want to make a quick note here on this point. What is so alluring to the church leaders of today, that they would completely overlook the amazing exchange that Christ makes in us and for us through salvation?

We preach hell as being hot. We preach humanity as being depraved. We preach that not one of us is good (Romans 3:12). Preachers have no problem calling out the pre-salvation wicked hearts of men.

But when a person recognizes this and becomes a new creation in Christ, many churches don't spend any time helping this new believer discover the deep well of righteousness that has been bestowed upon them by our benevolent Heavenly Father. We miss an entire portion of the gospel message here, and it baffles me where the disconnection is in today's church leadership climate.

No wonder we shy away from holiness, good works, sanctification, and manifestations of the Holy Spirit in the lives of the church. When you remove this piece of righteousness from the gospel message, you stunt the growth of the believer and then blame God for something He has not done.

Received, Not Earned

Some have argued that this type of teaching and thinking is prideful and promotes self-righteousness. I simply don't see that at all. What is prideful and self-righteous about accepting what God says about me? If God puts significance on me, then how does me acknowledging His love get twisted to be prideful?

I think it's prideful and falsely humble to deny the very things God has given. Pride is defined as arrogant and self-promoting. When I receive from God His gift of righteousness through faith, and this drives me to walk confidently in obedience to His Word, He is pleased, and it honors Him. It points people to Him. Pride and confidence are entirely different.

It seems others think that living in my identity in Christ somehow takes away from the glory of God. Living out my identity in Christ does not take away from who God is. As a matter of fact, it celebrates His heart for His children. He is still sovereign and supreme. We are His offspring and carry His nature and show His glory through our transformed lives (Acts 17:28). When I walk in my identity with God and reflect His image, He is glorified.

Self-righteousness is putting my trust in my own ability and striving to be right by my own ways. Receiving the righteousness of God by faith is a biblical gospel response (Romans 4:3; Philippians 3:9; Hebrews 11:7). Love is freely given, not earned. However, love must also be received for it to have any effect. God has freely given His love, and if I choose to receive that love, it will manifest fully in my life.

I think some people are so afraid of abusing God's Word that they never step out in faith in response to His promises. Hebrews 11:6 says that God is pleased by our faith. A true biblical understanding of faith is that it is active. Faith by definition is not idle. Walking a life of faith is a requirement for a disciple of Christ. Faith can only come by and through God's Word, and when we latch on to His Word and have a confident expectation that what it says is true, we are pleasing God and taking Him at His Word.

In the chapters ahead, we will look at many examples of self-righteousness and unrighteousness, but we will focus on what the Bible says specifically about our righteousness in Christ. When you begin with your identity, "the way you are," and then you open the Scriptures to try to affirm your identity, instead of following God's plan for your identity, you are asking Him to honor something that He has not blessed.

God is the only One who can define you. Your identity should be swallowed up in His identity. He loves you where you are, in spite of where you currently find identity. Then, that love then transforms you into His image, moving you away from any other false identity.

He loves you too much to allow you to stay where you are. He intends greater revelation and transformation for you as you learn to abide in your new identity in Him.

Chapter One Questions

Question: Why do you think most churches focus more on a person's sinful state apart from Christ rather than on a believer's righteous state with Him? How would it change your life if you truly believed that righteousness is for now and not just for eternity?

_____

_____

_____

_____

_____

_____

_____

_____

_____

_____

_____

_____

_____

Action: Define *righteous*, *unrighteous*, and *self-righteous*.

_____

_____

_____

_____

_____

_____

_____

_____

_____

_____

_____

Question: What pictures come to mind when you hear the word *righteous*? Write your "first impressions" of what righteousness looks, sounds, and acts like. As you continue this study, observe which of your ideas are based on cultural expectations or man-made rules, and which are based on the Scriptures.

_____

_____

_____

_____

_____

_____

_____

_____

_____

_____

_____

_____

Action: Read Appendix A to learn about the STAR journaling process. Plan to journal using the prompts at the end of each chapter.

Journal: For your first STAR journal entry, read and meditate on 2 Corinthians 5:21 and follow the STAR journal process. What does it mean for you to be the righteousness of God in Christ?

Chapter One Notes

CHAPTER TWO

Are We Preaching
Only Half of the Gospel?

We have somehow got hold of the idea that error is only
that which is outrageously wrong; and we do not seem to
understand that the most dangerous person of all is the
one who does not emphasize the right things.[7]

—**D. Martyn Lloyd-Jones**

Men are apt to prefer a prosperous error, to an afflicted
truth.[8]

—**Jeremy Taylor**

The purpose of this book is to help you replace your
current identity by abiding in your identity in Christ and
living in righteousness. If I can help you to expose some
hidden underlying embedded theology, then you can build
on the proper foundation throughout the rest of this book
and abide in your true identity in Christ.

In a 1990 interview with PBS, Billy Graham himself stated his belief that only about 25 percent of those who came forward at one of his events actually became Christians. In recent years, studies have shown that only 6 percent of people who "come forward" at an evangelistic crusade are any different in their beliefs or behavior one year later.[9]

Sadly, this means that there was no internal transformation for these folks. There was only outward conformation and an emotional experience that caused them to pursue Jesus for only a moment.

The human heart is complex, and the human condition is not an easy obstacle to overcome. So, what do we do with this reality? How should this affect our pursuit of righteousness? How should this affect how we live out our faith and reach the lost? And what does it mean for how we handle those who would teach otherwise?

Twisted Scripture

There are many false teachers and those straying away from the foundational teachings of Christianity, and we need to be watchful. The New Testament talks quite a bit about those who will come from the outside of the church and those who will rise up from within the church to deceive and draw many away unto themselves (1 Timothy 4:1–2; 2 Timothy 4:3–4). The false teachers are typically easy to identify and stay away from. It is the ones who seem to be teaching half-truths who make it difficult. Many sincere teachers are not willingly leading others astray but only teach half of the gospel. They stop short of the fullness of righteousness that Christ intends for you. You must be careful to discern and rightly divide the Word of Truth. Learn to self-feed on God's Word and not simply take others' word for what God is trying to teach you. All throughout the Bible, there are examples of people who chose to take God at His Word and those who chose to ignore, twist, or disobey the words of God. Those who obeyed God saw His promises fulfilled in their lives, and those who rejected God did not. It seems that there are two main reasons why people do not walk with the Word of God in their lives.

My people are destroyed for lack of knowledge. Because you have rejected knowledge, I also will reject you from being priest for Me; because you have forgotten the law of your God, I also will forget your children.

—Hosea 4:6

This verse in Hosea mentions two reasons for the destruction of God's people—a lack of knowledge and a rebellion against the knowledge they already had.

A Lack of Knowledge

For they being ignorant of God's righteousness, and seeking to establish their own righteousness, have not submitted to the righteousness of God.
—Romans 10:3

The word *ignorant* is not as bad of a word as some think. Ignorance simply means a lack of knowledge. To be ignorant means you simply don't have an understanding about something. So many people do not walk in the promises of God because they have not been taught or they have been taught wrong. As is mentioned in the verse above, sometimes well-intentioned people make bad choices for a lack of knowing. This is sometimes referred to as a sin of omission instead of commission. This gives the quote above huge significance. If you are not taught and/or discover the full truth, you can be deceived into ignoring God's Word or focusing on the wrong things. If you are not aware of the righteousness of God available for you, then how can you abide in it? Either way, the promises of God go unfulfilled for you.

Acts of Willful Rebellion

The second reason is the act of commission of sin. This is willful disobedience, or rebellion. Many know the Word of God, but they choose to deny it and simply do what pleases them. This act of disobedience will stagnate and kill the promises of God in your life. If you are going to abide in your identity in Christ, you must not be ignorant of His purpose and word for your life, and you must learn to quickly obey once you know what He asks you to do.

When you don't walk in the righteousness of God, you will easily fall prey to ignorance of His promises as well as rebellion against His words. The children of Israel in the book of Judges were not intimately connected to the

Lord firsthand but had only heard from the previous generation about Him. This led to their ignorance and ultimate rebellion against God's desires (Judges 2:7–14). This is why understanding this topic is crucial for your spiritual maturity.

> *Now the serpent was more cunning than any beast of the field which the Lord God had made. And he said to the woman, "Has God indeed said, 'You shall not eat of every tree of the garden'?"*
>
> *—Genesis 3:1*

"Did God Really Say?"

Half-truths can produce full-blown apostasy. One of Satan's earliest tricks was to get Eve to question the validity of God's Word. Eve was either not confident in what she knew to be true or she simply chose to disobey the direct command of God. If we are not careful to present the entire counsel of the Word of God, we leave people open to half-truths and deception.

In Numbers 13, the spies' perspective hardened the hearts of the people and lost an entire generation of promises. We must be careful how we learn, from whom we learn, and what we learn. Only half of the truth was shared. They assumed what the people of Canaan thought of them and projected that half-truth onto the people. This half-truth persuaded the crowd to reject Joshua and Caleb's report, and they turned their backs against the word that God had already given them about the land. This simple act of disobedience cost them an entire generation of people and withheld the promise of God until a later date.

When you take the text out of context, you are left with a con. As a steward of God's Word, you must carefully examine the Scriptures from an unbiased position within the context it has been given. When you do this, you should walk away with biblical truth in your heart and mind as it was intended to be interpreted and lived out.

I am continually amazed at how many sincere teachers of the Word only point people to who they were prior to Christ. It's as if their theology stops after salvation. They talk about grace and redemption, but they teach as if they want people to live under the law and the bondage of sin. It's as if they miss the entire message of grace, new birth, transformation, and new life in Christ.

Please don't misunderstand me. The depravity of humans before Christ is a part of the evangelistic gospel message that needs to be proclaimed to the lost. Yes, we lived apart from Christ. But there is also hope. This is just the beginning of the full message of transformation.

A Message of Hope and Love

Once you have been found by Christ, there is a different message that God gives us in His Word. You are born again, and your nature is changed—the previous covenant becomes fulfilled and you are now under a new and better covenant (Hebrews 12:24; 2 Corinthians 5:17). This message is about discipleship, transformation, sanctification, holiness, and spiritual development. This message is about hope, and the fruits and gifts of the Holy Spirit

(Galatians 5:22–23; 1 Corinthians 12). This message is one of an adoptive Father who has brought you into His holy kingdom and put you in heavenly places in Christ Jesus (Ephesians 2:4–7; Romans 8:12–17). This message is a love story of God bestowing upon you His righteousness. If you leave this part of the gospel out, then you are only preaching half of the gospel. While we don't come to Christ for the benefits, why would we deny all the benefits that God shows us are a part of the life of a new covenant believer?

If we simply go back to the book of beginnings and see the significance and worth that God put on humanity, Adam and Eve, we can see His heart for mankind. God was not shy in celebrating the gift of man that He had created in His image and likeness. He declared His creation as good (Genesis 1:26). In other places, we see how God puts significance and worth on humanity.

See the fullness of the gospel message and how God sees you. Throughout the rest of this book, I will continually point you to what the Bible says about you and your position with God as a child of His. I want you to see the heart of a loving God drawing you into an intimate, abiding relationship with Him. This is what so many in the church and the world are longing for but missing.

How Did You Come to Christ?

Coming to Christ affects how you live for Him. Your understanding of God and what brought you to salvation is a huge part of how you will look at your sanctification and your future relationship with God.

I will list a few ways in which I have seen the modern-day church culture call people to salvation. I am painting with a broad brush here and simply giving an overview to help you see how these lines of thinking can lay a foundation of unrighteousness that never allows you to abide in your identity in Christ. This is not meant to be critical or exhaustive. I simply want to make the point that how you come to Christ greatly affects how you live for Him, or how you don't.

I have many friends in different denominations, with different doctrinal beliefs and networks. Many of us disagree on some theological issues, but we can agree on the foundational Christian doctrines. What we do agree on is what unites us. We may simply see different biblical interpretations on what that looks like. Much of what we disagree on we have done so through loving, respectful conversations and dialogue over many years. Please understand that my heart here is not to offend or divide. In my personal circles, we don't allow our disagreements to break our friendship and fellowship. We are better together when we debate. We understand that truth travels best on the road of relationship when we don't argue. Instead, iron sharpens iron (Proverbs 27:17).

Hand in the Air

This is very common in many evangelical circles. Many people hear a message on how hot hell is, how all their woes and trials will disappear in heaven, or how rich you will become if you walk down the aisle. They simply see God as their ticket to get out of hell and into heaven.

They see God as a spiritual Santa Claus or a slot machine, and it selfishly motivates them to make an emotional decision. While I don't doubt some have made sincere life commitments to God in settings like this, I question the larger, long-term fruit that comes from this type of focus. Don't confuse a onetime, emotional, "hand in the air" with a sincere call to gather around an altar and seek the Lord, pray, repent, and cry out to God. The latter involves personal abandonment and seeking God, while the former is more of a mere glance at the true path to salvation.

In my experience with this type of "hand in the air" altar call, there was little contemplation of the gospel message before a decision was made. There was very little opportunity for people to count the cost as Jesus directs us to do. Many people in settings like this are simple consumers, and they remain unaware of the gravity of sin, their need for a Savior from sin, and the repentance necessary to compel them to turn away from their sin and toward a holy God. They are simply responding to a self-centered, *what's in it for me* type of call. Many people I know who have simply walked an aisle in response to an altar call have experienced little or no life transformation. They come under a false pretense and then become disillusioned when life does not magically change in their favor. When they come up against biblical doctrine that calls them to the hard work of obedience, holiness, and transformation, they reject that as legalism.

Where do you see this type of "easy" call to salvation in the Bible? There are certainly biblical examples of large crowds gathered and preached to with a message of repentance. However, the big difference is that the biblical examples include a call to repentance and the commitment to a life of discipleship, not just a onetime response. In other words, the people didn't experience a onetime crusade, but rather a call to discipleship, dying to self, and life transformation.

I have had dozens of people ask me why they were never taken through discipleship but only asked to walk an aisle one time. Many with whom I have walked through discipleship over the years get upset and feel betrayed when they see the biblical context of salvation, righteousness, lordship, obedience, holiness, transformation, and discipleship for the first time. They feel like they only got half the gospel. On the contrary, I have never had someone in a discipleship context upset that I didn't simply have them walk an aisle for their call to salvation. They see the biblical call to discipleship, personal abandonment, and absolute trust. They are grateful and appreciative that someone took the time to go beyond a onetime call to repentance.

To be clear, the preached and proclaimed gospel message is still a vital part of the church. My concern is, what are they being preached unto? After they hear the message and their heart is moved upon to repentance, what is asked of them? What follow-up is given? What discipleship is in place to grow them in their walk with Christ?

Here's a practical example I have used over the years: Most churches celebrate someone walking down an aisle. We cheer and shout on the day they get baptized. We then give them a book and sign them up for a four-week class, and then we ask them to be a good Christian.

This would compare to a hospital environment where babies are being born. We go into the delivery room. The family gathers around and shouts and hollers at the new life that is just born. We wrap the baby up in a blanket and then move into the next room to see the next one born. This makes no sense. Someone needs to take that baby and nurture him or her into adulthood. The baby will have long-term care needs that mean the difference between death and life for them.

It's the very same way in the spiritual realm. We are called to do more than have people walk aisles. We must make disciples of them (Matthew 28:19). We must commit to these spiritual newborns, to care for them until Christ forms spiritual maturity in them, until they understand this message of abiding in righteousness.

If we neglect this portion of our calling in the church, we are doomed to have a bunch of spiritually adolescent people walking around in physical adult bodies. Or worse yet, we may have a group of deceived people thinking they are saved but who only have a form of godliness. How they came to Christ is how they will live for Him. We will see very little commitment, and little if any transformation. Instead, a consumer mentality will keep them spiritually immature.

Checking the Boxes

This invitation to salvation comes in the form of good works, confirmation of completed ordinances, classes, intellectual learning, and other forms of self-righteous behaviors. Many in this type of environment are introduced to a pattern of conforming to sets of standards. They thrive on external conformation but see very little internal transformation, if any. This pattern bleeds over into their sanctification, and they never fully grasp true righteousness.

Groups in these camps thrive on church attendance, outreach events, social justice campaigns, and other things that motivate good feelings within people. All of these things can be good if they are done as a fruit of transformation, and not as a means of righteousness. There is a fine line here. Many I have talked with over the years in church environments like this will say the reason they do good works is because it makes them feel good. They argue that their good works will outweigh the bad works and that God will accept them based on these works. They are not working out biblical prescriptions in obedience to Christ out of a transformed heart. Rather, they are doing what makes them feel good. Good works motivate them. They are trying to be saved by their good works.

O foolish Galatians! Who has bewitched you that you should not obey the truth, before whose eyes Jesus Christ was clearly portrayed among you as crucified? This only I want to learn from you: Did you receive the Spirit by the works of the law, or by the hearing of faith? Are you so foolish? Having begun in the Spirit, are you now being made perfect by the flesh? Have you suffered so many things in vain—if indeed it was in vain? Therefore He who supplies the Spirit to you and works miracles among you, does He do it by the works of the law, or by the hearing of faith?
—Galatians 3:1–5

Like the people in the Galatian church, many in these camps will acknowledge that they cannot save themselves. They will have a sincere moment of repentance and find salvation. However, they will live their entire Christian walk with a tainted view of righteousness. Although they were saved by grace through faith, they will try to live their sanctification by works (Ephesians 2:8). How they came to Christ has totally overshadowed how they live for Christ.

Election by God

Many subscribe to a theology that God pre-selected a group to be saved and a group to be damned. There is a wide spectrum on this specific topic that can lead to almost endless research and study. You can get so caught up in the intellectual processing of this topic that you can miss the very life of God in the midst of all the knowledge. Many of this mindset believe that you have no say in your salvation. God chooses, and you are either in or out. If God selects you, you cannot reject Him, and if He rejects you, you cannot choose Him. Many teach that mankind is so depraved that we cannot make a response to salvation without God electing us. This belief limits, or removes altogether, human free will from the conversation and puts everything on the sovereignty of God.

While there is much to be debated and discussed on this point, my study does not lead me to this conclusion. The Bible has too many examples of the open celebration of the heart of God, which desires all to come into His kingdom. God is sovereign, and I fully embrace and love that.

However, like with other terms, we must define what *sovereign* means if we are going to truly walk in it. I see a God revealed in Scripture who, in His sovereignty, gave humanity, from Adam on, a free will to either choose His love or reject it. My biblical understanding actually points to a destiny provided that invites humanity into an intimate, abiding relationship with God. Not because we have no choice, but because His love has given us a choice. Love that is forced or required is not love at all. This is the very essence of this book. God is pure and holy and cannot mix with sin. He loves us so much that He has provided a way of removal from sin and entrance into His kingdom. This provision comes with a choice to either walk in or reject His gift. The fact that He has given you a choice shows His love for you.

If you have no choice in your salvation, then you certainly won't mysteriously make a change and start taking responsibility for your choices and walk in obedience after salvation. Some extreme views along these lines involve a refusal to evangelize or pursue holiness. Just today I was listening to a prominent teacher who subscribes to a form of this doctrine. He was saying almost exactly what I am saying here. He was teaching that no matter what he does or does not do, God has already chosen him, and so his daily decisions involving holiness, obedience, and sanctification were not up to his will, but only up to the hand of a sovereign God. He gave himself a clear "out," a scapegoat allowing him to live a life outside of any personal responsibility. This teacher is loved by many and has a huge following.

Another fruit of this type of thinking I have seen is what I call a "bastard mentality." A bastard is someone who is estranged from a loving, caring parental environment, or an illegitimate child. In my experience, many who subscribe to an extreme election theology have a hard time accepting the fact of being in right standing with God. They consistently feel unworthy, inferior, abnormal, and orphaned. This is not the adoptive spirit that the Bible promises. How they came to God plays into how they view their relationship with God. How they came to Christ has stunted their ability to see the righteousness that Christ bestows on them. They don't accept the love and grace of God as that of a loving Father, but rather are only a predetermined number that has little or no significance.

Grace Through Faith

Having faith for salvation is a foundational pattern for having faith in other areas of our Christian walk. The same faith in response to the gospel for salvation is the same faith we appropriate toward other promises in God's Word. When we don't accept any personal action in response to the gospel message but only put it off on God, we start a pattern that is typically repeated in other areas of our Christian walk. Many people in today's Christian church came to Christ with the understanding that God did everything, and they did nothing.

This line of thinking removes or limits the free will of man. It teaches that God has not given humanity free will but only predestined everything and everyone's choices. As with much biblical revelation, I subscribe to the idea that it's simple. While it's not as easy to live out, it's not complicated, either. Many people complicate very simple topics that can become stumbling blocks to others. I like what D.A. Carson said: "There are some forms of stupidity that one must be highly intelligent and educated to achieve."[10] More complicated does not equal more spiritual.

Why are some people so afraid to acknowledge the wonderful gift of free will from God? I see in Scripture where God continually sets choices before people and asks them to make a decision.

I have heard Bible teachers use the example of Adam and Eve to show God's original design for marriage, sexuality, creation, and a whole host of other topics. They have no problem using this as a prescriptive design of God. Yet, when it comes to the topic of free will, they won't allow the recorded text to speak with the same authority. I think we can look to the first created humans and see God's design, intention, and prescriptions, and then grow our thinking from there.

When God created humanity and placed them in the garden, He gave them several important things. He gave them the principle of seedtime and harvest, work, and purpose. He also gave them authority (Genesis 1:28). With this authority came freedom to make choices. He placed a tree from which He told them not to eat, and yet they did. He allowed them free choice. We see this concept played out throughout the entire Bible from that point on.

Let's get back to the grace-through-faith conversation. You cannot do anything to earn your salvation, however; you must act on the invitation before it becomes alive in your life. If you received the grace of God by faith, then you did something in response to the free gift. Again, I am not saying at all that you did anything to earn it, only receive it. *Faith* in the New Testament is an action word. Faith that is not active is dead (James 2:20). Active faith responds to God's Word. When you respond, there was an action on your part. In my opinion, assuming that God was the only One involved in your salvation is just as destructive and deceptive as people teaching that we can earn our righteousness by our good works. They both fall on extreme sides of sound biblical teaching. Received, not earned, is what I am trying to get across here.

If I were to offer two people each a check for one million dollars simply because I was benevolent, this would be a free gift. Neither of the two people did anything to earn my benevolence. The gift was simply a token of my love toward them without any work on their part. That is like the gift of salvation from God. He offers this free gift to everyone based on His goodness and love and not on our works or worth.

However, there is a huge piece to this equation that is so important to study. If I offered two people each a check for one million dollars simply because I was benevolent, and only one of those two accepted the check, then only one of those two will walk in the benefits of the gift. Please understand this vital concept. *Simply accepting the gift was an action and showed intention, movement, and choice, but it was not earned.*

Did the person who accepted the gift do something to receive the gift? Yes, they had to willfully participate in the accepting of the free gift. They had to cash the check and apply the benefits to their own life. Did the person who accepted the gift earn the gift? No, the gift was freely and benevolently given. There was nothing done to earn the gift. In the words of writer Dallas Willard, "Grace is not opposed to effort; it's opposed to earning."[11]

We need to stop teaching that people have no part in their salvation or that you did nothing as it pertained to your own salvation. You absolutely did something, and this begins a pattern of walking in the promises of God in salvation, sanctification, obedience, and holiness. You didn't earn anything, but you clearly, actively walked in faith toward God's promise.

For by grace you have been saved through faith, and that not of yourselves; it is the gift of God, not of works, lest anyone should boast.
—Ephesians 2:8–9

In the verses from Ephesians 2 listed above, if you remove faith from the equation, you are left with grace that has not been applied to the person's life. If grace was not received through faith, then that person is still dead in their trespasses and sin.

This is a simple explanation of the gift of salvation. None of us can earn the grace of God or gift of salvation, but for this gift to be active in our lives, we must receive it through faith. It is an act of our will that activates the gift of salvation for us. This simple process of thought can free you up and bring accountability to you in the area of salvation, as well as the areas of spiritual development and transformation.

Our salvation is not earned, just like our progressive sanctification, or righteousness, is not earned. They are all received as free gifts from God and then walked out with fear and trembling with God (Philippians 2:12). Sanctification, obedience, holiness, and a whole host of other things are fruits of a transformed heart. You cannot work them up, force them, or earn them. You must receive them as a fruit of abiding in Christ. Again, how you come to God affects how you live for Him. If you do not learn to appropriate the promises of God by faith in your life, starting with salvation, you will not walk in the fullness of your identity in Christ.

Here are a handful of other passages of Scripture that affirm the active faith on our part that initiates grace in our lives.

But without faith it is impossible to please Him, for he who comes to God must believe that He is, and that He is a rewarder of those who diligently seek Him.
—Hebrews 11:6

This scripture reminds us that God requires faith in the life of a disciple. This verse speaks to the act of coming to God, and then it says that this person must have faith. If we have nothing to do with our salvation, then why do this verse and many other passages of Scripture put acts of faith as a prerequisite to walking in the promises of God?

...knowing that a man is not justified by the works of the law but by faith in Jesus Christ, even we have believed in Christ Jesus, that we might be justified by faith in Christ and not by the works of the law; for by the works of the law no flesh shall be justified.

—Galatians 2:16

Our works do not justify us, but we must actively walk in faith to receive the promise of justification.

...just as Abraham "believed God, and it was accounted to him for righteousness."

—Galatians 3:6

Abraham's act of belief allowed him to walk in the righteousness of God.

Abraham believed God, and it was accounted to him for righteousness."

—Romans 4:3

Therefore it is of faith that it might be according to grace, so that the promise might be sure to all the seed, not only to those who are of the law, but also to those who are of the faith of Abraham, who is the father of us all...

—Romans 4:16

For the wrath of God is revealed from heaven against all ungodliness and unrighteousness of men, who suppress the truth in unrighteousness...

—Romans 1:18

If men are able to suppress the truth of God, it shows an act of their will. Romans 1 clearly talks about people knowing God through His creation but willfully rejecting His grace and receiving the penalty of their actions.

For I am not ashamed of the gospel of Christ, for it is the power of God to salvation for everyone who believes, for the Jew first and also for the Greek. For in it the righteousness of God is revealed from faith to faith; as it is written, "The just shall live by faith."
—Romans 1:16–17

Therefore, having been justified by faith, we have peace with God through our Lord Jesus Christ, through whom also we have access by faith into this grace in which we stand, and rejoice in hope of the glory of God.
—Romans 5:1–2

For indeed the gospel was preached to us as well as to them; but the word which they heard did not profit them, not being mixed with faith in those who heard it.
—Hebrews 4:2

The verse above is powerful. The same gospel was preached, but it was only the one who took the knowledge and applied faith that got any benefit.

But as many as received Him, to them He gave the right to become children of God, to those who believe in His name.
—John 1:12

The word "right" here is *exousia* in the Greek, meaning power, authority, weight, especially: moral authority.[12] We have the authority to call ourselves a child of God! Again, we are talking about appropriating the promise of righteousness of God in our life. If you don't have the full truth about this, you will neglect to walk in the fullness of your identity. I encourage you to carefully study these many scriptures and let them speak the value of God over you. Step out in faith and receive the fullness of your identity in Him. Don't allow anything to stand in the way of full righteousness in Christ. Don't settle for half of the gospel truth and live deceived.

The Ministry of a Priest, Apostle, Spiritual Father, or "Go Between"

Many people come to Christ in organizations that promote the idea that you have to have a spiritual leader as your access to Christ. This person is said to have a special calling, authority, or relationship with God that you need in order to gain entrance. This idea is, unfortunately, abused in a lot of religious circles. People come with the expectation that anytime they want access to God, they must come through an earthly host.

If you came to Christ with the understanding that you need a priest or a pastor (outside of Christ), then that idea will potentially stunt your growth and discipleship. This is extremely frustrating to me, as so many people have been deceived and are not walking in their righteous identity in Christ because of these half-truths. God has put in place church leaders for many purposes and we absolutely need them. However, we must let God be the one who defines what we need them for.

Therefore, holy brethren, partakers of the heavenly calling, consider the Apostle and High Priest of our confession, Christ Jesus...

—Hebrews 3:1

For there is one God and one Mediator between God and men, the Man Christ Jesus...

—1 Timothy 2:5

Jesus is the Great High Priest (Hebrews 4:14–16). This role of Christ places great significance on those for whom He intercedes. He knows us intimately, and that shows our significance. If anyone ever tells you that you need them or whatever they are selling to get to God, then run as fast as you can. When you are in the righteousness of God, there is nothing that stands between you and Him. You have full access all the time.

Seeing then that we have a great High Priest who has passed through the heavens, Jesus the Son of God, let us hold fast our confession. For we do not have a High Priest who cannot sympathize with our weaknesses, but was in all points tempted as we are, yet without sin. Let us therefore come boldly to the throne of grace, that we may obtain mercy and find grace to help in time of need.

—Hebrews 4:14–16

I don't know how it could be any clearer. You have access to the throne of grace through your High Priest, Jesus Christ.

I would even include in this conversation certain ordinances of the church, like communion and even corporate preaching and teaching. I know many professed Christians who will not repent of sin unless they do it to a church leader, priest, or around a church-sanctioned communion table. They have been taught that their relationship with Christ is dependent on certain gifts and forms or it is not accepted. This is so disappointing and confusing. This type of teaching is half-true and leads people away from abiding in their true identity. Part of your intimate, abiding relationship with Christ is the access of living in a posture of repentance. You don't need a church leader or a communion table to do that. You have access to the throne of grace at all times, especially in your time of need.

This includes the topic of self-feeding. I have heard church leaders say that the average Christian is just a dumb sheep and not capable of a viable relationship with God without the help of a pastor. They go as far as to say that Christians must have a church leader teach them, feed them spiritually, and interpret Scripture for them. They believe that only ordained ministers have the gift and understanding from God needed to administer certain aspects of the Word of God. I don't understand why a church leader would put so much pressure on his/her role in this way. These half-truths cause a lot of people to only feed on God's Word in a corporate church gathering or while listening to a podcast. They never dive in to the

Scriptures to get vertical revelation directly from God. They rely on a pastor or leader to direct their spiritual feeding, and this is a half-truth.

One of the greatest expressions of love I can give a new believer is to teach them to self-feed on God's Word and cultivate an enjoyable prayer life. Church leaders can and should teach, preach, and make disciples. This should be in addition to teaching self-feeding and intimacy with Christ. I believe the number one role of a church leader is to connect the head, Christ, to the Body. This is where transformation happens. This is where righteousness is experienced. When we cloud that up with ordinances of man, we are in danger of deceiving those whom Christ has trusted us with, and that is dangerous ground.

> *Then the brethren immediately sent Paul and Silas away by night to Berea. When they arrived, they went into the synagogue of the Jews. These were more fair-minded than those in Thessalonica, in that they received the word with all readiness, and searched the Scriptures daily to find out whether these things were so.*
> **—Acts 17:10–11**

This group of Bereans did not swallow all that the apostle Paul and Silas were teaching. They received the word, but they used it as a supplement to their personal fellowship with Christ. They searched the Scriptures to hold accountable the words they were hearing.

Another amazing gift that Christ has given us as we abide in our true identity is the person of the Holy Spirit. There are volumes of books that are written on this one, but I want to give a few verses that speak to the power of the Spirit.

> *But the anointing which you have received from Him abides in you, and you do not need that anyone teach you; but as the same anointing teaches you concerning all things, and is true, and is not a lie, and just as it has taught you, you will abide in Him.*
>
> *—1 John 2:27*

> *And I will pray the Father, and He will give you another Helper, that He may abide with you forever—the Spirit of truth, whom the world cannot receive, because it neither sees Him nor knows Him; but you know Him, for He dwells with you and will be in you.*
>
> *—John 14:16–17*

> *I still have many things to say to you, but you cannot bear them now. However, when He, the Spirit of truth, has come, He will guide you into all truth; for He will not speak on His own authority, but whatever He hears He will speak; and He will tell you things to come. He will glorify Me, for He will take of what is Mine and declare it to you. All things that the Father has are Mine. Therefore, I said that He will take of Mine and declare it to you.*
>
> *—John 16:12–15*

> *But as it is written: "Eye has not seen, nor ear heard, nor have entered into the heart of man the things which God has prepared for those who love Him." But God has revealed them to us through His Spirit. For the Spirit searches all things, yes, the deep things of God. For what man knows the things of a man except the spirit of the man which is in him? Even so no one knows the things of God except the Spirit of God. Now we have received, not the*

spirit of the world, but the Spirit who is from God, that we might know the things that have been freely given to us by God. These things we also speak, not in words which man's wisdom teaches but which the Holy Spirit teaches, comparing spiritual things with spiritual. But the natural man does not receive the things of the Spirit of God, for they are foolishness to him; nor can he know them, because they are spiritually discerned. But he who is spiritual judges all things, yet he himself is rightly judged by no one. For "who has known the mind of the Lord that he may instruct Him?" But we have the mind of Christ.

—1 Corinthians 2:9–16

Rise Above

...as His divine power has given to us all things that pertain to life and godliness, through the knowledge of Him who called us by glory and virtue, by which have been given to us exceedingly great and precious promises, that through these you may be partakers of the divine nature, having escaped the corruption that is in the world through lust.

—2 Peter 1:3–4

Don't let any manmade ways to Christ get in the way of how you were intended to experience Him. Don't allow half-truths to keep you from all that God has for you. Be like the Bereans, who searched the Scriptures to affirm what was being said to them. When you get hold of these revelations and abide in your identity, your life will never be the same. You have all that you need to abide in righteousness.

Chapter Two Questions

Question: Give examples of how the way someone initially received salvation might affect their understanding of righteousness and their growth in Christ.

_____

_____

_____

_____

_____

_____

_____

_____

_____

_____

_____

Question: What does it mean that salvation is by "grace through faith"? Why is this so vital? Does your church teach this clearly, or does it put too great an emphasis either on works to the exclusion of grace, or on God's sovereignty to the exclusion of faith?

_____

_____

_____

_____

_____

_____

_____

_____

_____

_____

_____

Action: Write out a testimony of how you came to Christ. Evaluate whether or not you accepted some unbiblical ideas or half-truths when you received your salvation. Talk through with a mentor or accountability group how these wrong ideas may be affecting your present walk.

_____

_____

_____

_____

_____

_____

_____

_____

_____

_____

_____

_____

_____

Journal: Read and meditate on Ephesians 2:8–10 and follow the STAR journal process. What is the role of each of these: grace, faith, God, you, works?

Chapter Two Notes

CHAPTER THREE

Identity Without Christ Versus Identity in Christ

Satan knows my name but calls me by my sin. God knows my sin but calls me by my name.

Who are you?

This is a common question that we ask in today's culture, and the answers are varied. "I am a..."

- husband or wife;
- employee or business owner;
- graduate, doctor, activist, philanthropist...

And the list goes on.

Usually in this string of defining qualities, we mention religion. We are Christians, Christ-followers, born again, Baptists, Catholics, believers. We drop this in among our other roles and responsibilities, and we treat it like it's just another responsibility, another quality that makes us who we are.

And yet it is the only quality that matters, for without it we are nothing. In this chapter, we will explore what the Bible says about your identity *without Christ* and then who you are *in Christ*. We should look no further than God's Word to define us, and yet very few people do. Our tendency is to let other things in this world define us, including the enemy of our soul, Satan. We need to break out of our earthly, sinful identity and find our identity in Christ.

Who Are You Really?

When was the last time you examined your life? A mature believer learns to examine his life in light of the Word and what the Holy Spirit is revealing to him. However, I am asking you this question to provoke you to search your soul for an honest answer. Much like a doctor would perform a physical exam, conduct a spiritual and soul examination on yourself. If I came to you and I sat down in an examination room and asked the following questions, what would your responses be?

- Who are you?
- Why on earth are you here?
- What is your identity?
- What is your purpose?

How would you respond?

Rick Warren published a book in 2002 titled *The Purpose Driven Life*.[13] As of 2017, more than thirty-three million copies in over 50 different languages had been sold globally.[14] In this book, he asked this simple question and then explained it biblically: "Why on earth am I here?" Why do you think so many people bought copies of this book? I think it's because every one of us is asking the same question, whether we know it or not. Why on earth am I here? What is this all about? Who am I?

It would be good for you to take a minute and reflect on these questions and see what comes to mind. What answers did you come up with? Many people would answer these questions with responses like: how many kids they have; their ethnicity or religion; whether they are married or single; where they work; whether they are vegan, vegetarian, or a meat lover. Some might talk about their sexuality. You might talk about your favorite sports team, or whether you're a musician or an actor. You might mention what your favorite thing is in life.

Whatever your answer is to these questions says a lot about what you are identifying with. Many people, when I ask what they relate to, start getting into the "what" instead of who they are and why they exist.

As humans, we all want to belong. One core need of all human beings is acceptance. God created us this way. However, He creates us to find our acceptance in Him. We are so desperate for love and acceptance that many times we will choose bad love and bad acceptance. When you don't understand biblically defined righteousness, it is easy to find your identity in horizontal, earthly things.

Years ago, I read that if a person does not worship God, that does not mean they worship nothing. In actuality, they will worship anything and everything.[15] This can lead you down many paths that will detract from the blueprint that God has for your life.

As a disciple of Christ, one of your greatest joys should be your identity in Christ. If you find your identity today in anything outside of Christ, then you are not experiencing the fullness of abiding in His identity. Let's take a look at what our identity is before Christ and what it looks like after we become His disciples.

Jesus has given you His identity, and He says you should be hidden with Him in God (Colossians 3:3). You should find your existence in Him. The reason you wake up in the morning, the reason you breathe in and breathe out, is because Christ has set your life in motion and you exist for His purpose and for His glory. The Bible says He created all things through Him, for Him, and for His glory (Colossians 1:16). So, where do you fit into all of this?

Unrighteous

Before you come to Christ, the identity that you have is bleak and depressing. According to the Bible, we are all born into the human race with the sin nature that was introduced to us by the first Adam (Romans 5:12). We have no choice in the matter. This seed is our nature and drives our sinfulness. This has many devastating implications, but the most damning of all is that this sin separates us from a holy God.

Contrary to popular belief, humans are not born good,

nor are we all children of God. These are two very popular falsehoods that are being promoted even in Christian churches today. The Bible is clear that as human beings, we are all created in the image of God (Genesis 1:23). We are all loved by God. However, we are not all children of God. Only those who are born again are His children (John 1:12).

Sin marred the image of God in humanity. When Jesus rose from the dead, He provided redemption for all who would come His way. Redemption was not automatically given to all mankind in one instant but simply provided for. Why do so many want to use the argument that we are all made in the image of God and are all children of God, and yet in the same breath they refuse to submit themselves to Him? If you admit you are made in His image, then you admit there is a supreme deity, and that should bring you pause and cause you to humbly submit yourself to Him.

Our identity before Christ is that we are by nature children of wrath, slaves of sin, our father is Satan, and we are destined to eternal separation from God. We are hopeless (Ephesians 2:3). There is nothing that we can do to save ourselves; we are in dire need of a savior. Our identity is expressed in our fleshly desires. We are driven and destined to fulfill our fleshly desires at the expense of anyone or anything that gets in our way. This does not sound very appealing, nor should it.

It is important to understand the depth of sin's consequences. Many in the church today miss this important part of the gospel. We try to gloss over the wickedness and hopelessness that our lives are filled with when we are outside of Christ. Part of the beauty of the gospel is the depth of sin from which God delivers you. If you don't recognize your sinfulness, you will never look for a savior. If you don't understand the power of sin and depravity, you will not appreciate the fullness of righteousness. You cannot be saved if you first do not acknowledge your need for Christ. You cannot save yourself. There is no good work or abstinence of bad works that will be good enough to redeem you from sin.

Here are just a few verses that drive this point home. As you read these scriptures, look at the identity that you have outside of Christ. Examine the depth of depravity that is prevalent in the human race. Let the gravity of what is being said sink in as you read each passage.

Outside of Christ, there is not much hope when you come to the conclusion that these four verses express. I am a sinner, a slave to sin, and I have fallen short. As a result of my sin, there are many consequences, but the most glaring punishment is the kind of death that separates me from a holy God.

Jesus answered them, "Most assuredly, I say to you, whoever commits sin is a slave of sin."
—John 8:34

...for all have sinned and fall short of the glory of God...
—Romans 3:23

For the wages of sin is death...
—Romans 6:23a

Do you not know that the unrighteous will not inherit the kingdom of God? Do not be deceived. Neither fornicators, nor idolaters, nor adulterers, nor homosexuals, nor sodomites, nor thieves, nor covetous, nor drunkards, nor revilers, nor extortioners will inherit the kingdom of God. And such were some of you.

—1 Corinthians 6:9–11a

The following verses continue to expose the depth of my sin and the increasing list of consequences. My sinful nature gives place to fleshly works that are anything but godly. I have no control to possess my vessel but give way to lustful expression. My sin continues to build its case against me, leaving me no hope on the basis of my works in the flesh.

Now the works of the flesh are evident, which are: adultery, fornication, uncleanness, lewdness, idolatry, sorcery, hatred, contentions, jealousies, outbursts of wrath, selfish ambitions, dissensions, heresies, envy, murders, drunkenness, revelries, and the like; of which I tell you beforehand, just as I also told you in time past, that those who practice such things will not inherit the kingdom of God.
—Galatians 5:19–21

...in which you once walked according to the course of this world, according to the prince of the power of the air, the spirit who now works in the sons of disobedience, among whom also we all once conducted ourselves in the lusts of our flesh, fulfilling the desires of the flesh and of the mind, and were by nature children of wrath, just as the others.
—Ephesians 2:2–3

Therefore put to death your members, which are on the earth: fornication, uncleanness, passion, evil desire, and covetousness, which is idolatry. Because of these things the wrath of God is coming upon the sons of disobedience, in which you yourselves once walked when you lived in them.
—Colossians 3:5–7

...that each of you should know how to possess his own vessel in sanctification and honor, not in passion of lust, like the Gentiles who do not know God...
—1 Thessalonians 4:4–5

The more I read, the further my conviction seems evident. I seek no other interest but self-gratification and self-preservation. My selfish tendencies take control of my ability to manage my life, and I find my identity taking on words like *abominable, godless, idolater,* and *hopeless.*

For men will be lovers of themselves, lovers of money, boasters, proud, blasphemers, disobedient to parents, unthankful, unholy, unloving, unforgiving, slanderers, without self-control, brutal, despisers of good, traitors, headstrong, haughty, lovers of pleasure rather than lovers of God, having a form of godliness but denying its power.
—2 Timothy 3:2–5a

To the pure all things are pure, but to those who are defiled and unbelieving nothing is pure; but even their mind and conscience are defiled. They profess to know God, but in works they deny Him, being abominable, disobedient, and disqualified for every good work.
—Titus 1:15–16

*For we have spent enough of our past lifetime in doing the
will of the Gentiles—when we walked in lewdness, lusts,
drunkenness, revelries, drinking parties, and abominable
idolatries.*

—1 Peter 4:3

I once thought that my managed behaviors could produce a self-righteousness that would save me from
my sin. However, now my conclusions are all driving
toward unrighteousness. My good deeds certainly do
not outweigh the evil that is present within me. What
can I do to be saved from this wickedness that is
within me?

*What then? Are we better than they? Not at all. For we
have previously charged both Jews and Greeks that they
are all under sin. As it is written: "There is none righteous,
no, not one; There is none who understands; there is none
who seeks after God. They have all turned aside; they have
together become unprofitable; there is none who does
good, no, not one." "Their throat is an open tomb; with
their tongues they have practiced deceit"; "The poison of
asps is under their lips"; "Whose mouth is full of cursing
and bitterness." "Their feet are swift to shed blood; Destruction and misery are in their ways; and the way of
peace they have not known." "There is no fear of God before
their eyes." Now we know that whatever the law says, it
says to those who are under the law, that every mouth may
be stopped, and all the world may become guilty before
God. Therefore by the deeds of the law no flesh will be justified in His sight, for by the law is the knowledge of sin.*

—Romans 3:9–20

Now the full gravity of my depravity is crushing me under its heaviness. I see that a holy God's wrath is against me. This holy God has condemned me to punishment for the sin in which I live. Is there not an escape from this unrighteousness?

For the wrath of God is revealed from heaven against all ungodliness and unrighteousness of men, who suppress the truth in unrighteousness, because what may be known of God is manifest in them, for God has shown it to them. For since the creation of the world His invisible attributes are clearly seen, being understood by the things that are made, even His eternal power and Godhead, so that they are without excuse, because, although they knew God, they did not glorify Him as God, nor were thankful, but became futile in their thoughts, and their foolish hearts were darkened. Professing to be wise, they became fools, and changed the glory of the incorruptible God into an image made like corruptible man—and birds and four-footed animals and creeping things. Therefore God also gave them up to uncleanness, in the lusts of their hearts, to dishonor their bodies among themselves, who exchanged the truth of God for the lie, and worshiped and served the creature rather than the Creator, who is blessed forever. Amen. For this reason God gave them up to vile passions. For even their women exchanged the natural use for what is against nature. Likewise also the men, leaving the natural use of the woman, burned in their lust for one another, men with men committing what is shameful, and receiving in themselves the penalty of their error which was due. And even as they did not like to retain God in their knowledge, God gave them over to a debased mind, to do those things which are not fitting; being filled with all unrighteousness, sexual immorality, wickedness, covetousness, maliciousness; full of envy, murder, strife, deceit, evil-mindedness; they are whisperers, backbiters, haters of God, violent, proud, boasters, inventors of evil things, disobedient to parents, undiscerning, untrustworthy, unloving, unforgiving, unmerciful; who, knowing the righteous judgment of God, that those

*who practice such things are deserving of death, not only
do the same but also approve of those who practice them.*
—Romans 1:18–32

*He who believes in Him is not condemned; but he who does
not believe is condemned already, because he has not believed in the name of the only begotten Son of God. And this
is the condemnation, that the light has come into the
world, and men loved darkness rather than light, because
their deeds were evil.*
—John 3:18–19

Wow! How desolate and hopeless. It is not a pretty picture when you take humanity's sin nature at face value.
This is a grim reality that many in the church either do not
understand or they miss the other side of depravity—
righteousness. If you have never acknowledged your sinfulness to God, repented, and made Him Lord of your life,
I encourage you to do so now. If you need further instruction, contact a local church pastor or contact our ministry
through our website: www.abidingnetwork.com.

Identity in Christ

If I mention that I'm a servant of God, some will say they
aren't servants, they're friends. If I say I am a friend of
God, some will say they are not friends, but sons. If I say
I'm a son of God, some will say they are not sons, they are
a part of the Bride of Christ. If I say I am part of the Bride
of Christ, some will say they are not; they are a part of the
body of Christ on earth. Each point can be successfully
argued from Scripture. The error is not theological. It is
in the heart—it's the inability to recognize and value the

lessons that others are learning in Christ. The insecure often find their security in having an opinion that differs from others'.[16]

—Bill Johnson

I will use the rest of this book to set forth a biblical blueprint that combats the unrighteousness you just read about. The chapters ahead will open wide the door for you to abide in your identity in Christ. This is where it gets exciting, as you explore the love the Father has for you and that He expressed in Christ. His righteousness was accredited to you, and you get to abide in that. My prayer is that you experience the joy abiding in your identity in Christ.

Three men were sitting at a bus stop. Rain poured down, but their small area under the awning was dry.

The first man had a bag of belongings at his feet. He was unshaven. He looked at the rain and exclaimed, "Praise God. He loves me enough to give me shelter!"

The second man wore a fast-food uniform. He looked at the rain and said, "Praise God I don't have to walk to work today!"

The third man wore a suit and clutched a briefcase. He took one look at the rain and said, "Praise God my SUV broke down earlier when it wasn't raining!"

The three men might have all been waiting at the same bus stop for the same bus, yet they each saw how God had cared for them and shown love to them in unique ways.

Each of us has a unique relationship with God. The sooner we stop comparing ourselves to others or to what we think God wants us to be, the sooner we can begin to find our identity in Him.

In Christ, we are slaves to righteousness and our Father is God. The Holy Spirit gives life where the law once brought death (Romans 8:2). We are adopted into the family of God and our identity changes immediately (Romans 8:14–17). Just like you did not earn your salvation but only receive it, walking in your new identity is the same way. You simply have to receive your new nature and begin to appropriate it by faith. The Bible tells us that faith comes from hearing the Word of God (Romans 10:17). In response to that, I am going to list a portion of the hundreds of love letters from God that He has given to you in His Word. I ask that you prayerfully self-feed on each of these until they become a part of who you are. Meditate on these words of life. Allow your identity to be defined and swallowed up by what God says about you.

John 8:31–36 reminds you that you are free. You do not have to be a slave to sin, unrighteousness, or self-righteousness any longer.

Then Jesus said to those Jews who believed Him, "If you abide in My word, you are My disciples indeed. And you shall know the truth, and the truth shall make you free." They answered Him, "We are Abraham's descendants, and have never been in bondage to anyone. How can You say, 'You will be made free'?" Jesus answered them, "Most assuredly, I say to you, whoever commits sin is a slave of sin. And a slave does not abide in the house forever, but a son abides forever. Therefore if the Son makes you free, you shall be free indeed."

Ephesians 2:1–10 tells you that when you are born again, you are no longer dead in sin but alive in Christ. You do not have to participate in your former conduct. That conduct is for the unrighteous. You are the righteousness of God in Christ, and you are here on earth to do good things for His glory.

And you He made alive, who were dead in trespasses and sins, in which you once walked according to the course of this world, according to the prince of the power of the air, the spirit who now works in the sons of disobedience, among whom also we all once conducted ourselves in the lusts of our flesh, fulfilling the desires of the flesh and of the mind, and were by nature children of wrath, just as the others. But God, who is rich in mercy, because of His great love with which He loved us, even when we were dead in trespasses, made us alive together with Christ (by grace you have been saved), and raised us up together, and made us sit together in the heavenly places in Christ Jesus, that in the ages to come He might show the exceeding riches of His grace in His kindness toward us in Christ Jesus. For by grace you have been saved through faith, and that not of yourselves; it is the gift of God, not of works, lest anyone should boast. For we are His workmanship, created in Christ Jesus for good works, which God prepared beforehand that we should walk in them.

Second Corinthians 5:17–21 reminds you of who you used to be before Christ. Now, as a new creation, you are an ambassador of Christ, claiming righteousness. God expresses His love and goodness to the world through you.

Therefore, if anyone is in Christ, he is a new creation; old things have passed away; behold, all things have become new. Now all things are of God, who has reconciled us to

*Himself through Jesus Christ, and has given us the ministry
of reconciliation, that is, that God was in Christ reconciling
the world to Himself, not imputing their trespasses to
them, and has committed to us the word of reconciliation.
Now then, we are ambassadors for Christ, as though God
were pleading through us: we implore you on Christ's behalf, be reconciled to God. For He made Him who knew no
sin to be sin for us, that we might become the righteousness
of God in Him.*

Galatians 3:26–29 is an important reminder that nothing should divide us Christ-followers. Not race, politics,
social status, class status—we are all equal heirs. When
you look at others in the body of Christ, you can have joy
that we are all unified in the righteousness of Christ. There
should be no competition or disunity.

*For you are all sons of God through faith in Christ Jesus.
For as many of you as were baptized into Christ have put
on Christ. There is neither Jew nor Greek, there is neither
slave nor free, there is neither male nor female; for you are
all one in Christ Jesus. And if you are Christ's, then you are
Abraham's seed, and heirs according to the promise.*

Colossians 3:8–10 says that we are to bear the image
of Christ. This asks us to forget our old ways and put on
our new selves. Did you know that in Christ you actually
will reflect the image of Christ? You are newly created in
Him. Are you starting to see the power of abiding in your
identity? If you will get this revelation, it will transform
you forever.

But now you yourselves are to put off all these: anger, wrath, malice, blasphemy, filthy language out of your mouth. Do not lie to one another, since you have put off the old man with his deeds, and have put on the new man who is renewed in knowledge according to the image of Him who created him...

Remember everything that we waded through earlier in this chapter? It was not pretty to see who you are outside of Christ. It was not pretty to be reminded of how sin kept you separate and distant from God. Now look at who you are in Christ. Colossians 1:12–14 makes it clear that you are delivered from darkness and you have been forgiven and redeemed. Now you have been qualified to be a partaker of this inheritance.

...giving thanks to the Father who has qualified us to be partakers of the inheritance of the saints in the light. He has delivered us from the power of darkness and conveyed us into the kingdom of the Son of His love, in whom we have redemption through His blood, the forgiveness of sins.

Remember all of the verses earlier in this chapter that reminded you of how you were a slave to sin? Sin dominated your nature and every decision you made. Now contrast that with the fact that Romans 6:1–8 reminds you that you are united with Christ. You are to live with Him, free from sin.

What shall we say then? Shall we continue in sin that grace may abound? Certainly not! How shall we who died to sin live any longer in it? Or do you not know that as many of us as were baptized into Christ Jesus were baptized into His death? Therefore we were buried with Him through baptism into death, that just as Christ was raised from the dead by the glory of the Father, even so we also should walk in newness of life. For if we have been united together in the likeness of His death, certainly we also shall be in the likeness of His resurrection, knowing this, that our old man was crucified with Him, that the body of sin might be done away with, that we should no longer be slaves of sin. For he who has died has been freed from sin. Now if we died with Christ, we believe that we shall also live with Him...

First John 5:11–13 is a precious promise that you are to have eternal life. You no longer have to worry about what tomorrow brings. This promise allows you to simply abide in your identity now and in eternity.

And this is the testimony: that God has given us eternal life, and this life is in His Son. He who has the Son has life; he who does not have the Son of God does not have life. These things I have written to you who believe in the name of the Son of God, that you may know that you have eternal life, and that you may continue to believe in the name of the Son of God.

Romans 8:1–4 reminds us that Christ made a way for us to walk by the Spirit, not by the flesh. This is another wonderful reminder that you do not have to be dominated by that old sinful nature. You can live in the Spirit, outside of any condemnation.

There is therefore now no condemnation to those who are in Christ Jesus, who do not walk according to the flesh, but according to the Spirit. For the law of the Spirit of life in Christ Jesus has made me free from the law of sin and death. For what the law could not do in that it was weak through the flesh, God did by sending His own Son in the likeness of sinful flesh, on account of sin: He condemned sin in the flesh, that the righteous requirement of the law might be fulfilled in us who do not walk according to the flesh but according to the Spirit.

First Corinthians 6:9–11 holds special meaning for me. When I preach at Catalyst Church on this topic of righteousness, I note all of the places where Scripture compares where we "once were" to where we "are now" in Christ. Years ago, when I was preaching on righteousness and reading the scripture above, I reached the "once were … but now are" part and said, "We love big 'buts' at Catalyst Church."

I sincerely did not realize how that sounded when it came out, and everyone got a good laugh. I had to change the verbiage to "big conjunctions" instead of "big buts." I use this as an illustration so that hopefully you will always remember the power of this message. Earlier in this book, we saw what we are like outside of Christ and it's not pretty. Now we get the joy of basking in who we are in Christ. This is your identity. Learn to walk in it with confidence and boldness.

Do you not know that the unrighteous will not inherit the kingdom of God? Do not be deceived. Neither fornicators, nor idolaters, nor adulterers, nor homosexuals, nor sodomites, nor thieves, nor covetous, nor drunkards, nor revilers, nor extortioners will inherit the kingdom of God. And such were some of you. But you were washed, but you

*were sanctified, but you were justified in the name of the
Lord Jesus and by the Spirit of our God.*
—1 Corinthians 6:9–11

Ephesians 5:8–10 challenges us to walk in the light,
seeking that which is pleasing to God. When you abide in
your identity in Christ, your desires change and produce
in you a hunger and thirst for His righteousness.

*For you were once darkness, but now you are light in the
Lord. Walk as children of light (for the fruit of the Spirit is
in all goodness, righteousness, and truth), finding out what
is acceptable to the Lord.*

Philippians 1:6 is a beautiful reminder that Jesus is
continually working on us.

*...being confident of this very thing, that He who has begun
a good work in you will complete it until the day of Jesus
Christ...*

Philippians 3:12–14 tells us that we are getting closer
to the goal every day.

*Not that I have already attained, or am already perfected;
but I press on, that I may lay hold of that for which Christ
Jesus has also laid hold of me. Brethren, I do not count myself to have apprehended; but one thing I do, forgetting
those things which are behind and reaching forward to
those things which are ahead, I press toward the goal for
the prize of the upward call of God in Christ Jesus.*

Finally, Romans 6:17–19 proclaims the truth that we are now slaves of righteousness.

> *But God be thanked that though you were slaves of sin, yet you obeyed from the heart that form of doctrine to which you were delivered. And having been set free from sin, you became slaves of righteousness. I speak in human terms because of the weakness of your flesh. For just as you presented your members as slaves of uncleanness, and of lawlessness leading to more lawlessness, so now present your members as slaves of righteousness for holiness.*

Do you feel the love God has for you? He knows your struggle, He knows this life is difficult, and He has made a way for you to get through it. Even now, Jesus is working on bringing you out of your old ways and closer to Him, and your role is to accept it. Accept it and chase after it with everything you have. Abide in your identity.

WORKBOOK

Chapter Three Questions

Question: When you hear the question "Who are you?" what immediately comes to mind? How do you describe yourself on social media accounts or when meeting a new friend? From where are you most apt to draw your identity?

_____

_____

_____

_____

_____

_____

_____

_____

_____

_____

_____

Question: Describe the condition of a person apart from Christ. What was your life like before salvation? What might your life look like now if you had never been saved?

_____

_____

_____

_____

_____

_____

_____

_____

_____

_____

_____

Question: What is your identity in Christ? Looking at the verses in this chapter, write out a list titled "In Christ I Am..."

_____

_____

_____

_____

_____

_____

_____

_____

_____

_____

_____

_____

_____

Journal: Meditate on Galatians 5:16–26 and follow the STAR journal process. Does your life reflect one that is abiding in Christ or one that is apart from Him?

Chapter Three Notes

CHAPTER FOUR

Which Covenant Are You Living Under?

We have all heard it said, "You can lead a horse to water, but you can't make him drink." One wise farmer added, "But you can put salt in the oats." This is how God uses the Old Testament Law, or covenant, in our lives; it's "salt in our oats" to make us thirsty for a righteousness that is not ours. I think this is an important chapter because it can help you remain vigilant against falling into self-righteousness. Unrighteousness and self-righteousness will keep you from abiding in His righteousness.

The Pharisees tried to make friends with the Law and pretend to obey it. By doing this, they could justify themselves and feel good about "their" holiness. The result was minimization of the Law. They turned God's Law into a code of conduct relating to only external behaviors. They could only handle it on a human level: washing hands, fasting, doing various ceremonial deeds three times a day. They avoided the issues of the heart: justice, mercy;

faithfulness, love, etc. They could not live up to those demands in their own strength. The Law was reduced to a legalistic set of rules that devout Pharisees could manage without any help, even God's. This was a perversion of the purpose of the Law.

The problem is that some of us are still doing this today. We are doing all the outward "activities," and we are neglecting the inward journey.

If you don't understand covenant and how serious God takes the idea of covenant, you will never fully abide in the benefits that come with being in covenant with Him. Throughout human history, God instituted and authored testaments, or covenants, and He is the keeper and finisher of them. Too many New Covenant believers are still trying to live under the Old Covenant and hanging around the outer courts while neglecting to enter the holy place where God has created them to dwell.

Let's look at some of the Old Testament covenants so that you can see the significance of the New Covenant of grace we are living under. This New Covenant produces a righteousness that was not available under the Old.

Creation, Fall, and Promise of a Redemption Covenant

The story of creation reveals so much about God's heart and design for mankind (Genesis 1:26–31; 2:15–25). God created male and female in His image and likeness. God placed them in a sinless environment and gave them authority to rule the place of their dwelling. God walked and talked openly with humanity at this point because there was no sin hindering the relationship. God's glory clothed humanity, and shame was not felt. This design is how God intended the relationship with Him and humanity to always be. Nothing hindering their righteousness in Him.

Satan enticed Adam and Eve to go against the command of God, and in doing so, all of creation was cursed (Genesis 3:1–24). As you read the Bible from cover to cover, you see the depths of depravity that sin's curse produced. The greatest fruit of sin was the separation that sin caused between man and God. Humanity could no longer commune with God as they once did. The righteousness that they once had was gone, and the image of purity was marred. God made a promise to humanity and to Satan that He had a plan to fix the problem and would reveal it at a later time. In that moment, God shed the blood of an innocent animal and covered the humans with its skin. This was a foreshadowing of the Mosaic covenant that God would give hundreds of years later.

Noahic Covenant

Then the Lord saw that the wickedness of man was great in the earth, and that every intent of the thoughts of his heart was only evil continually. And the Lord was sorry that He had made man on the earth, and He was grieved in His heart. So the Lord said, "I will destroy man whom I have created from the face of the earth, both man and beast, creeping thing and birds of the air, for I am sorry that I have made them." But Noah found grace in the eyes of the Lord.

—Genesis 6:5–8

The people of the earth were consumed with wickedness, and God decided to destroy mankind, minus Noah and his family. God provided a way of deliverance for them while judgment consumed the rest of the earth. God is so good to always bring a way of deliverance to His people. Once again, this covenant was not the final solution for sin. This covenant was only a foreshadowing of what was coming.

God entered into a covenant with Noah and his family. You can read more about this in Genesis 6–9. The sign of God's covenant with Noah was the rainbow. Many have taken this sacred sign and made a mockery of it in today's culture. However, every time you see a rainbow, it should encourage you, because God is expressing this sign of the covenant with Noah.

Abrahamic Covenant

You can read about this more in Genesis 12–25, but I will highlight the covenant portion here for our discussion.

> *Now the LORD had said to Abram: "Get out of your country, from your family and from your father's house, to a land that I will show you. I will make you a great nation; I will bless you and make your name great; And you shall be a blessing. I will bless those who bless you, and I will curse him who curses you; And in you all the families of the earth shall be blessed."*
>
> *—Genesis 12:1–3*

And it came to pass, when the sun went down and it was dark, that behold, there appeared a smoking oven and a burning torch that passed between those pieces. On the same day the LORD made a covenant with Abram, saying: "To your descendants I have given this land, from the river of Egypt to the great river, the River Euphrates—the Kenites, the Kenezzites, the Kadmonites, the Hittites, the Perizzites, the Rephaim, the Amorites, the Canaanites, the Girgashites, and the Jebusites."

—Genesis 15:17–21

When Abram was ninety-nine years old, the LORD appeared to Abram and said to him, "I am Almighty God; walk before Me and be blameless. And I will make My covenant between Me and you, and will multiply you exceedingly." Then Abram fell on his face, and God talked with him, saying: "As for Me, behold, My covenant is with you, and you shall be a father of many nations. No longer shall your name be called Abram, but your name shall be Abraham; for I have made you a father of many nations. I will make you exceedingly fruitful; and I will make nations of you, and kings shall come from you. And I will establish My covenant between Me and you and your descendants after you in their generations, for an everlasting covenant, to be God to you and your descendants after you.

—Genesis 17:1-7

As with other covenants, this was not the final covenant with humanity that would eradicate the sin problem. This covenant involved God's separating a people that would be for His name and for His glory. This people group is a posterity in the earth even to this day.

One of the amazing things about Abraham was that he was a man of faith, and God accounted his faith as righteousness (Romans 4:9). This is not the fullness of righteousness that we have access to today, but a type of it. You can read more about this in Hebrews 11 and Romans 4.

Mosaic Covenant-Law

In the third month after the children of Israel had gone out of the land of Egypt, on the same day, they came to the Wilderness of Sinai. For they had departed from Rephidim, had come to the Wilderness of Sinai, and camped in the wilderness. So Israel camped there before the mountain. And Moses went up to God, and the Lord called to him from the mountain, saying, "Thus you shall say to the house of Jacob, and tell the children of Israel: 'You have seen what I did to the Egyptians, and how I bore you on eagles' wings and brought you to Myself. Now therefore, if you will indeed obey My voice and keep My covenant, then you shall be a special treasure to Me above all people; for all the earth is Mine. And you shall be to Me a kingdom of priests and a holy nation.' These are the words which you shall speak to the children of Israel." So Moses came and called for the elders of the people, and laid before them all these words which the Lord commanded him. Then all the people answered together and said, "All that the Lord has spoken we will do." So Moses brought back the words of the people to the Lord. And the Lord said to Moses, "Behold, I come to you in the thick cloud, that the people may hear when I speak with you, and believe you forever."

—Exodus 19:1–9

(For the full context, read Exodus 19–24.)

After 430 years, the family of Abraham had become the nation of Israel. When God gave the Mosaic Covenant to Moses, He was not nullifying His previous covenant, but adding to it for a very clear purpose.

What Does This Mean for Today?

Now that we've gone over some examples of old covenants, we can see how beautiful and important they were in their time. They were deeply meaningful, but God never intended for them to be used today to replace a relationship with Him. As it says in 1 Timothy 1:8, "We know that the law is good if one uses it properly" (NIV).

But how can we take these old laws and properly use them in today's culture? How can we look at the commands and promises of God and not let our faith become like the Pharisees'?

The proper use of the Law accomplishes at least three things. It's through these three things that we can determine how to best handle and utilize covenant law without turning it into something that God didn't intend it to be.

The Proper Use of the Law Reveals Sin

Through the Law, we become conscious of sin. We see more clearly our sinfulness and the holiness of God (Romans 3:20). The Pharisees believed the Law was given for us to live up to it. So, when they felt they accomplished it, they were righteous and justified. But Jesus set the standard much higher than this.

Therefore, by the deeds of the law no flesh will be justified in His sight, for by the law is the knowledge of sin.
—Romans 3:20

I would not have known I was a sinner without the law.
—Romans 7:7

The Law was a grave reminder of our inability to be self-justified before God. No matter how hard you try, you will never be able to live up to all that the Law requires. This reveals our sin.

The Proper Use of the Law Produces Brokenness

The next purpose of the Law is to convince you that in no way possible can you keep the Law. Coming to God in your righteousness will not work. This exposes your need for a savior. The Law is a grave reminder of the power of sin and your inability to accomplish the demands of the Law. The Law shows the condemnation that is upon each of us because of our sin and the consequences associated with sin.

We learn this in the passage right after the Beatitudes. (For a deeper look into Jesus' teaching on the Beatitudes, see the conclusion of the book as well as my book *Abiding at the Feet of Jesus*.) In Matthew 5:17–30, Jesus is using the Law properly. He says, "You haven't committed murder, but you have been angry. You haven't committed adultery, but you have lusted." Jesus wasn't saying, "Come on, guys, try harder, shape up!" He was saying, "Look inside your hearts where your anger, rage, and lust live. There is no way you can keep the whole Law." This is what happens when confronted with the full force of the Law. After striving, you get tired. This leads you to a humble brokenness that says, "I cannot do this in my own strength."

If you are honest with brokenness at this point, you will begin to search for a solution to your sin problem. You will acknowledge that in all of your trying and failing that you are worse off than when you started. This is what the Law was meant to do. Reveal sin and produce brokenness. It is salt to make us thirsty. Thank God that He did not leave us hopeless. He gave all of this to point to His solution.

The Proper Use of the Law Will Drive You to Christ

For the law, having a shadow of the good things to come, and not the very image of the things, can never with these same sacrifices, which they offer continually year by year, make those who approach perfect. For then would they not have ceased to be offered? For the worshipers, once purified, would have had no more consciousness of sins. But in those sacrifices, there is a reminder of sins every year. For it is not possible that the blood of bulls and goats could take away sins.

—Hebrews 10:1-4

The Law was never given to remove sin, only to cover offenses and be a reminder of our wickedness. A thorough study of this topic would take many more chapters than we have to offer. Remember, this is only an overview to get a point of reference for the covenant we are invited to live in. When the priests would make a yearly atonement for the sins of the people, it was a reminder of the sin. This was a time of grave reflection and serious focus. Under the Law of Moses, sin was not cleansed fully. Sin was simply covered with the blood of bulls and goats. The sin problem was still there. But the Law offered hope that another, better covenant was coming.

> *What purpose then does the law serve? It was added because of transgressions, till the Seed should come to whom the promise was made; and it was appointed through angels by the hand of a mediator. Now a mediator does not mediate for one only, but God is one. Is the law then against the promises of God? Certainly not! For if there had been a law given which could have given life, truly righteousness would have been by the law. But the Scripture has confined all under sin, that the promise by faith in Jesus Christ might be given to those who believe. But before faith came, we were kept under guard by the law, kept for the faith which would afterward be revealed. Therefore the law was our tutor to bring us to Christ, that we might be justified by faith. But after faith has come, we are no longer under a tutor.*
>
> **—Galatians 3:19–25**

Notice the use of the term *tutor* here. "Therefore the law was our tutor to bring us to Christ..." (Galatians 3:24). The most amazing thing to me about this picture is that the tutor is not the Teacher—instead, the tutor leads us *to* Him. The Lord wants His tutor, the Law, to drive us to His righteousness and grace. The Law reveals sin, produces brokenness, and drives us to Christ. When the Law has accomplished that, it doesn't result in self-righteous people. When it does its job, it produces people who are broken, who hunger and thirst for God.

Davidic Covenant

Now therefore, thus shall you say to My servant David, 'Thus says the Lord of hosts: "I took you from the sheepfold, from following the sheep, to be ruler over My people, over Israel. And I have been with you wherever you have gone, and have cut off all your enemies from before you, and have made you a great name, like the name of the great men who are on the earth. Moreover I will appoint a place for My people Israel, and will plant them, that they may dwell in a place of their own and move no more; nor shall the sons of wickedness oppress them anymore, as previously, since the time that I commanded judges to be over My people Israel, and have caused you to rest from all your enemies. Also the Lord tells you that He will make you a house. "When your days are fulfilled and you rest with your fathers, I will set up your seed after you, who will come from your body, and I will establish his kingdom. He shall build a house for My name, and I will establish the throne of his kingdom forever. I will be his Father, and he shall be My son. If he commits iniquity, I will chasten him with the rod of men and with the blows of the sons of men. But My mercy shall not depart from him, as I took it from Saul, whom I removed from before you. And your house and your kingdom shall be established forever before you. Your throne shall be established forever."

—2 Samuel 7:8–16

Many years later, a young man from the tribe of Judah within Israel became the king of this nation. God made a royal covenant with David that pointed the way for the family lineage of Christ. Through David and the covenant God established with him, the way was paved to build the tabernacle, where worship and prayer turned the nation back toward their coming King. This prepared the way for Christ's coming.

A New Covenant, a Covenant of Grace and Righteousness

Does God have a problem with the other covenants? No, He gave them. Covenants were His idea and His perfect way, because sin had distanced humanity from creation. God gave these covenants for a purpose and a season. I think we should learn and appreciate the process by which God chose the covenants and celebrate their history. Jesus did not abolish the Law but He fulfilled it and made it obsolete for the New Covenant believer. The tutor did what it was supposed to do; it led us to the Master. Let's move away from the tutor now and embrace our Master and Lord. Let's take some time to focus on the power of the New Covenant that has been given to us today.

But now He has obtained a more excellent ministry, inasmuch as He is also Mediator of a better covenant, which was established on better promises. For if that first covenant had been faultless, then no place would have been sought for a second. Because finding fault with them, He says: "Behold, the days are coming, says the Lord, when I will make a new covenant with the house of Israel and with the house of Judah—not according to the covenant that I made with their fathers in the day when I took them by the hand to lead them out of the land of Egypt; because they did not continue in My covenant, and I disregarded them, says the Lord. For this is the covenant that I will make with the house of Israel after those days, says the Lord: I will put My laws in their mind and write them on their hearts; and I will be their God, and they shall be My people. None of them shall teach his neighbor, and none his brother, saying, 'Know the Lord,' for all shall know Me, from the least

of them to the greatest of them. For I will be merciful to their unrighteousness, and their sins and their lawless deeds I will remember no more." In that He says, "A new covenant," He has made the first obsolete. Now what is becoming obsolete and growing old is ready to vanish away.
—Hebrews 8:6–13

A Better Covenant with Better Promises

When you gain the revelation of your true identity in Christ, so many of your decisions will change. It amazes me how many people do not appreciate the power and benefits of this better covenant. As we have seen in earlier places in this book, the Galatian church tried to accept the gift of the New Covenant and then live it out under Old Covenant principles. I see so many people in the body of Christ today doing the same thing. Abide in your identity and live in the fullness of the New Covenant.

Under the Old Covenant, you were not permitted direct access to God. God was distant and impersonal. You had to come through a priest, sacrifice, and rules. The Presence of God was housed in a tent or tabernacle that you were not allowed into. You could hang around the outer or inner court for ceremonial purposes, but never the holy of holies. This is a shell of what Christ has given you today. If you are born again, Christ has deposited the Holy Spirit, His very Presence, inside of you. No ceremonies. No outer court. You have full access at all times to God. This should change your appreciation of the New Covenant. You have the King of kings living inside of you. That sounds like a much better covenant to me! This is why it was so significant that when Christ died, the veil that kept people from the housed presence of God in the temple was torn in two from top to bottom (Matthew 27:51). This signified that under this new covenant, the presence of God was no longer found on stone tablets or in a building made with hands, but rather it was deposited into the hearts of believers.

> *Therefore, my brethren, you also have become dead to the law through the body of Christ, that you may be married to another—to Him who was raised from the dead, that we should bear fruit to God. For when we were in the flesh, the sinful passions which were aroused by the law were at work in our members to bear fruit to death. But now we have been delivered from the law, having died to what we were held by, so that we should serve in the newness of the Spirit and not in the oldness of the letter.*
>
> **—Romans 7:4-6**

Why in the world would you want to try to live under the old letter—the Old Covenant? This is the reason for this book. I want you to see the great gift of righteousness that has been bestowed upon you in Christ. Stop taking for granted this gift. With each new revelation comes a new dedication and consecration. Don't take this knowledge and live as you have in the past. Let this wind through your heart and mind. Live as a child of the King, empowered by His Spirit on the inside. This will change your entire being when you understand this. You have the authority, gifts, and fruits of the Holy Spirit, all of the things that pertain to life and godliness, access to the throne of grace, forgiveness of sins, the direction of the Holy Spirit, resurrection power, peace that surpasses your intellect, joy that is not able to be put into words, access to the Father God, and so much more. Why give up God's power by living under the Old Covenant?

Atonement Versus Justification

Earlier in this chapter, I wrote about sin being covered rather than being removed under the Old Covenant. While the atonement that was instituted under the Old Covenant held back God's wrath from the people, it never fully took away their sins. This is a powerful and key point to understand. John the Baptist, upon seeing Christ, declared, "Behold the Lamb of God who takes away the sins of the world." Taking away sin is much different from simply covering sin. This is another way the New Covenant is better than the Old.

Atonement can be defined as satisfaction given for a wrong committed. The person who committed the wrong still maintains the guilt, but the penalty has been removed. *Justification* is God's act of removing both the guilt and the penalty of sin while simultaneously presenting a sinner now justified and righteous before Himself. This person is no longer a sinner saved by grace, but a son upon whom righteousness has been bestowed.

Years ago, I heard this explained in a way that made great sense to me. Atonement is like a person who has been declared guilty in a court of law and sentenced to life in prison. However, a governor comes along and pardons the individual. A pardon does not erase the guilt of the crime you committed; it only offers forgiveness and removes the penalty. The record still shows that you are guilty of said crime. Justification is so much more. Justi-fication not only forgives the person and removes the penalty, but it also wipes out the guilt and any record of the crime committed. That is so powerful! God not only forgives us, but He restores us and declares us to be com-pletely righteous before Him. No Law or works could ever produce this. Only the grace and mercy of Jesus Christ.

> *For what the law could not do in that it was weak through the flesh, God did by sending His own Son in the likeness of sinful flesh, on account of sin: He condemned sin in the flesh, that the righteous requirement of the law might be fulfilled in us who do not walk according to the flesh but according to the Spirit.*
> **—Romans 8:3–4**

> *But now the righteousness of God apart from the law is re-vealed, being witnessed by the Law and the Prophets, even the righteousness of God, through faith in Jesus Christ, to all and on all who believe. For there is no difference; for all have sinned and fall short of the glory of God, being justi-fied freely by His grace through the redemption that is in Christ Jesus, whom God set forth as a propitiation by His blood, through faith, to demonstrate His righteousness, be-cause in His forbearance God had passed over the sins that were previously committed, to demonstrate at the present time His righteousness, that He might be just and the jus-tifier of the one who has faith in Jesus.*
> **—Romans 3:21–26**

The Greek rendering of the word *righteous* means "to show to be righteous, to declare righteous, acknowledged justice, justified, vindicated, and acquitted."[17] You are the righteousness of God in Christ; it is because of

Christ's great act on the cross that you are found not guilty.

> *Therefore, having been justified by faith, we have peace with God through our Lord Jesus Christ, through whom also we have access by faith into this grace in which we stand, and rejoice in hope of the glory of God.*
> **—Romans 5:1–2**

Righteousness restores a person to all that was lost at the fall of Adam, as well as brings us into a father/child relationship with God Himself.

> *For you did not receive the spirit of bondage again to fear, but you received the Spirit of adoption by whom we cry out, "Abba, Father." The Spirit Himself bears witness with our spirit that we are children of God, and if children, then heirs—heirs of God and joint heirs with Christ, if indeed we suffer with Him, that we may also be glorified together.*
> **—Romans 8:15–17**

The Law of Love

I believe that Jesus expressed the heart of God when He summed up the Law in the following way:

> *Teacher, which is the great commandment in the law?" Jesus said to him, "'You shall love the Lord your God with all your heart, with all your soul, and with all your mind.' This is the first and great commandment. And the second is like it: 'You shall love your neighbor as yourself.' On these two commandments hang all the Law and the Prophets."*

—Matthew 22:36–40

When you abide in your identity in Christ, you accept that love should be your response to people. This becomes a debt that you gladly give because you are operating out of a transformed heart.

> *Owe no one anything except to love one another, for he who loves another has fulfilled the law. For the commandments, "You shall not commit adultery," "You shall not murder," "You shall not steal," "You shall not bear false witness," "You shall not covet," and if there is any other commandment, are all summed up in this saying, namely, "You shall love your neighbor as yourself." Love does no harm to a neighbor; therefore, love is the fulfillment of the law.*
> *—Romans 13:8–10*

You also realize that love puts the needs of others above yourself. Servanthood becomes a joy to you as you model Christ, because your identity is wrapped up in Him.

> *For you, brethren, have been called to liberty; only do not use liberty as an opportunity for the flesh, but through love serve one another. For all the law is fulfilled in one word, even in this: "You shall love your neighbor as yourself."*
> *—Galatians 5:13–14*

But concerning brotherly love you have no need that I should write to you, for you yourselves are taught by God to love one another...
—1 Thessalonians 4:9

Righteousness allows you to fervently love others because you have experienced the tremendous power of love. Your response is to express that love to others, knowing that love covers so many things.

And above all things have fervent love for one another, for "love will cover a multitude of sin.
—1 Peter 4:8

Beloved, let us love one another, for love is of God; and everyone who loves is born of God and knows God. He who does not love does not know God, for God is love. In this the love of God was manifested toward us, that God has sent His only begotten Son into the world, that we might live through Him. In this is love, not that we loved God, but that He loved us and sent His Son to be the propitiation for our sins. Beloved, if God so loved us, we also ought to love one another. No one has seen God at any time. If we love one another, God abides in us, and His love has been perfected in us. By this we know that we abide in Him, and He in us, because He has given us of His Spirit."
—1 John 4:7–13

Are you starting to see the significance of this message? I hope you can see, at this point, the many angles from which the Bible reveals God's righteousness to you. I pray that your faith is building as your understanding increases. And I pray that your building faith will be expressed as you abide in your identity.

WORKBOOK

Chapter Four Questions

Question: What was the purpose of the Old Testament Law? How did the Pharisees (and others) distort that purpose? What does it mean that the Law is our tutor (but not our Teacher)?

_____

_____

_____

_____

_____

_____

_____

_____

_____

_____

_____

_____

Question: What are some ways that believers still try to keep an outward "law" while avoiding heart issues?

_____

_____

_____

_____

_____

_____

_____

_____

_____

_____

Question: What is the "Law of Love"? How is it practically lived out in a Christian's life?

_____

_____

_____

_____

_____

_____

_____

_____

_____

_____

_____

_____

Action: Write a list comparing and contrasting the Old and New Covenants. Include items such as access to God, dealing with sin, and position before God.

_____

_____

_____

_____

_____

_____

_____

_____

_____

_____

_____

_____

Journal: Meditate on Romans 8:1–4 and follow the STAR journal method. What are the promises for those who walk in the Spirit?

Chapter Four Notes

CHAPTER FIVE

Isn't the Heart Evil?

Blessed are the pure in heart, for they shall see God.
—Matthew 5:8

Under the New Covenant, we become new creations in Christ (2 Corinthians 5:17).[18] This includes our hearts, which are purified by Him. The essence of a pure heart is a heart that has been sifted and cleansed and has its affection fixed firmly on God.

God looks at you with love in His eyes. He created you in His very image and likeness. Sin marred that, which distorted the image. When you were born again, God restored the marred image and re-created you in newness of life. However, you look in the mirror and see the sinful person instead of the person into whom He has transformed you. But God is saying, "Look in the mirror of the Spirit of God and see that I truly created you in My likeness." This is such a powerful conversation that we must not gloss over it if we are going to abide in Christ and find our identity in Him.

God desires us to be broken in spirit and to have the beggarly dependence upon Him that will produce in us a mourning over our sin, and then ultimately repentance. This produces in us a meekness that is a soothing medicine and a gentle breeze—and a controlled power. That, in turn, produces in us an ability to both receive and give mercy. It produces a hungering and a thirsting, not after external religious things, but after the very righteousness of God.

Would you have the nerve to say that you have a pure heart before God? You're not alone if you aren't quick to jump up and holler, "Yes!"

How dare we say that we have a pure heart before God! Doesn't the Bible say that the heart is evil and wicked—that we are sinful people, and that only God is holy (Jeremiah 17:9)?

Yes, those are two true statements, but they aren't the whole story. This chapter will focus on what it looks like to have a pure heart before a holy, loving, and pure God.

Is the Heart Evil?

The heart is deceitful above all things, and desperately wicked; who can know it?

—Jeremiah 17:9

Who can say, "I have made my heart clean, I am pure from my sin"?

—Proverbs 20:9

To be honest, I have been amazed over the years how much misunderstanding surrounds the topic of our evil hearts. This is one area in which Satan has deceived so many in the Church. I have heard the verses above quoted over and over as an excuse as to why people cannot be held to a standard of holiness.

I argue that, not only can you have a pure heart, but that it is a requirement of a disciple. Not only can you be holy, but God expects it of you. Part of the gift of redemption is a pure heart. Living in your identity in Christ comes with purity of heart. Don't allow anyone to deter you from what God's Word says you can have or keep you from walking in it.

As much as the Bible tells us there is not one righteous and that the heart is evil, it also tells us that in Christ we can have a new heart and walk in the righteousness of God. What is this apparent contradiction all about? We know that sin keeps the unredeemed, human heart desiring things that are contrary to God. Now, let's examine what the new birth does in the human heart.

Defining the Terms

The best way I can describe this is to say that your spirit makes you who you are—it's what the Bible calls the inner person (2 Corinthians 4:16; 1 Peter 3:4; Ephesians 3:16). You have a soul that is comprised of your will, emotions, and understanding. All of this is housed in this earthly tent, the body (2 Corinthians 5:1). The spirit and soul are intimately connected and will exist forever. Many times, they are used interchangeably in conversation, but they are very different.

This fallen body is temporary, and when your spirit and soul are removed, your body will be lifeless. If you were to see me driving down the road and wave to me, would you yell out to your other neighbors, "There goes Nate's car"? No, you would simply say, "There goes Nate." It is the same way with our makeup. Your body simply houses the real you.

Heart, Soul, and Body

Let's look at a handful of scriptures that define the different aspects of our threefold, or three-part, nature. This is very important for you to learn in your life with Christ. To live in the fullness of your identity, you must learn to understand each aspect of your nature and navigate as the Bible directs.

Your human nature comprises a threefold existence:

> Now may the God of peace Himself sanctify you completely; and may your whole spirit, soul, and body be preserved blameless at the coming of our Lord Jesus Christ.
> **—1 Thessalonians 5:23**

> For the word of God is living and powerful, and sharper than any two-edged sword, piercing even to the division of soul and spirit, and of joints and marrow, and is a discerner of the thoughts and intents of the heart.
> **—Hebrews 4:12**

Your inner person is where God resides:

> *The spirit of a man is the lamp of the* LORD, *searching all the inner depths of his heart.*
>
> **—Proverbs 20:27**

Obedience comes from your inner person:

> *But God be thanked that though you were slaves of sin, yet you obeyed from the heart that form of doctrine to which you were delivered.*
>
> **—Romans 6:17**

When you are born again, God circumcises your heart and gives you a new heart because you are a new creation in Christ:

> *But he is a Jew who is one inwardly; and circumcision is that of the heart, in the Spirit, not in the letter; whose praise is not from men but from God.*
>
> **—Romans 2:29**

> *Therefore, if anyone is in Christ, he is a new creation; old things have passed away; behold, all things have become new.*
>
> **—2 Corinthians 5:17**

Your flesh is dying, but your inner person should be

renewed daily:

> *Therefore we do not lose heart. Even though our outward man is perishing, yet the inward man is being renewed day by day.*
> **—2 Corinthians 4:16**

Before we were saved, our hearts were wicked, our minds were evil, and our sinful nature led us to do what we pleased. When we were born again, our hearts were changed and became alive to Christ. We became new creations. The Holy Spirit does a re-creative work, and indeed we are now different. This is an immediate change that is glorious and amazing. We are empowered for godly living through the Holy Spirit.

> *And do not present your members as instruments of unrighteousness to sin, but present yourselves to God as being alive from the dead, and your members as instruments of righteousness to God. For sin shall not have dominion over you, for you are not under law but under grace.*
> **—Romans 6:13-14**

When you are born again, if you go and look in the mirror, you will not notice any physical changes. If you had gray hair, you still have gray hair. If you were tall or short, none of that changed. The new birth is not a physical change; it's an inner change. The Bible is clear that the sinful nature wants to indulge in fleshly things. You must learn to crucify your sinful desires, or these tendencies will dominate your life. Sin should not dominate you any longer.

At the same time, you still have a mind and emotions that have been trained to obey the demands of your desire. Every decision and action you made prior to rebirth was indulged in self-centered, sinful tendencies.

Many new believers are frustrated because they still feel the draw of the old nature, with its selfish thought patterns (Romans 7:13–25). This is all normal until you begin to allow the Holy Spirit to change you from the inside out. This transformation goes against everything you have ever known and experienced, and it can be painful.

Biblical Transformation

Consider the example of a wild horse. Think about the changes in thinking, habits, and intuition that would need to occur for this horse to be gentled. Before, he was responsible for finding food, water, and shelter. He ran where he wanted, protected himself when he was in danger, and could leap about wildly whenever he felt the urge.

As the horse is trained, he must learn to trust that his new master will provide him with a safe living environment. He is taught how to wear a restrictive bridle and to respond to commands. No longer can he buck and leap whenever he wants. It's not an easy process, is it?

As we become a "new creation," as 2 Corinthians 5:17 describes it, we must die to our sin natures, change our thinking, and begin responding to the Holy Spirit's promptings. Over time, this process of transformation and renewal of the mind will change us into the image of Christ (Romans 8:29).

What a powerful expression of transformation. God has given us complete liberty by imparting the Holy Spirit to us. He then proceeds to transform us into His image from one degree of glory to the next. In a true abiding relationship with Christ, this transformation will continue on an incremental basis and reveal more and more of God to us. At the same time, this will produce a change in our old man into Christ's likeness and image.

Learning to hear the Holy Spirit doesn't happen overnight. Just as a wild horse doesn't become docile the moment it steps into a stable, we don't flip a switch and suddenly have a transformed soul on a whim. Studying the Bible, being mentored by people who are spiritually mature, learning to self-feed on and apply God's Word in our lives, spending time in prayer, and fasting are all some of the ways in which God works to transform our souls.

Living with a Pure Heart

Although it seems unattainable, the necessity of a pure heart is undeniable. It is not just a suggestion—Jesus is emphatic in asserting, "Blessed are the pure in heart, for they will see God." Taken another way, that could mean that those who don't have pure hearts won't see God.

A pure heart is undivided, unmixed, unadulterated, sifted, genuine, and real, with no added mixture or element.

I think that one crucial element of having a pure heart is entering into a loving relationship with God. Imagine what would happen to a wild horse that is beaten by its master or isn't provided with good food. If the master was rough with the horse, it would never really become tamed. It might eventually obey out of fear, but the horse will still hold on to that wildness and possibly be a danger to the master and itself.

Jesus wants us to know that Kingdom life is a relational matter of the heart. And we can all get excited about that for one reason: We really do love God down deep in our hearts. We may stumble and fall at times, but the bottom line is that, in our hearts, we have a passion for Jesus and for the things of God. Despite our inconsistencies, there is still a determination to love Jesus with all of our hearts.

This was a problem for people both in the Old and the New Testaments. The one thing God cared about more than anything else was being deeply loved. And, this was the one thing people found most difficult to recognize.

When you think about it, it isn't hard to understand why. When I follow rules, I don't have to worry about my attitude. Imagine your preteen daughter emptying the dishwasher the way you asked her to, grumbling and rolling her eyes the whole time.

It's the same way with God. If I distance myself from a relationship with Him, I can conduct business ethically, not cheat on my wife, and go to church every Sunday while still enjoying my secret sin. I'm following the rules I want to follow, right? Therefore, I can excuse myself from being obedient in every area. When I don't bother to be close enough to my Heavenly Father to hear Him call me out on these issues, I don't have to look too closely at myself.

A Pure Heart Requires Faith

So, if actions alone don't create a pure heart, then what does? This is a question even the apostles had to sit and consider.

> *Now the apostles and elders came together to consider this matter. And when there had been much dispute, Peter rose up and said to them: "Men and brethren, you know that a good while ago God chose among us, that by my mouth the Gentiles should hear the word of the gospel and believe. So God, who knows the heart, acknowledged them by giving them the Holy Spirit, just as He did to us, and made no distinction between us and them, purifying their hearts by faith.*
>
> *—Acts 15:6–9*

First, a pure heart is received by faith. We see in Acts 15 that a debate had arisen in the early church. The problem had to do with the status of the new Gentile believers who had not yet been circumcised. Some were implying that the uncircumcised couldn't be saved. Peter answered them above with the reminder that God purified them in their hearts by faith, not by the work of circumcision (Acts 15:1–29).

If a pure heart is received by faith, then we must ask, "Faith in what?" We can't cleanse our own hearts. But by faith, we can experience the cleansing power of Jesus. We can ask for this pure heart. We can let God's grace in and receive it. We have clearly seen this in the progression of the Beatitudes.

> *"This is the covenant that I will make with them after those days, says the LORD: I will put my laws into their hearts, and in their minds, I will write them," then He adds, "Their sins and their lawless deeds I will remember no more." Now where there is remission of these, there is no longer an offering for sin.*
>
> **—Hebrews 10:16–18**

> *Then I will sprinkle clean water on you, and you shall be clean; I will cleanse you from all your filthiness and from all your idols. I will give you a new heart and put a new spirit within you; I will take the heart of stone out of your flesh and give you a heart of flesh. I will put My Spirit within you and cause you to walk in My statutes, and you will keep My judgments and do them.*
>
> **—Ezekiel 36:25–27**

A Pure Heart Requires the Holy Spirit

Second, the pure heart is implanted by the Holy Spirit. When, by faith, we receive the gift of salvation, we figuratively have a new heart implanted in us. In the verses above, we see that the prophet Ezekiel foretold a covenant that God would make through Christ, and this was mentioned again in Hebrews. This is the reason why the redeemed are not just people who learn the rules. This purification of our hearts is done through the gift of salvation.

It can be difficult for us to understand that purification of our hearts is both God's responsibility and our own. How can we say it's a gift and yet have to work for it?

I like to think of this as an apprenticeship. Once we, by faith, accept the gift of salvation, we are both absolutely new to Christianity and already accepted into God's kingdom. Jesus paid the price and gave us our identity, yet we have a long way to go before we have developed the skills we need to function maturely. This is the journey of discipleship.

Think back to that wild horse. It isn't expected to know how to respond to commands or how to handle a rider immediately. Yet, if it doesn't improve over time, there's something wrong.

Similarly, God knows that we are putting to death our sinful nature and learning to develop our "say no to self" muscles. Walking closely with Him will help us to grow stronger faster, help us to understand what He is calling us to do, and will make the sinful lifestyles we've lived in less appealing. Our hearts are growing more and more toward being pure, while all our sins are already forgiven.

Both Ezekiel and Hebrews celebrate the day when true believers can obey from pure hearts. The failure to recognize the need for a relationship rather than rules is one of the curses in churches today. Many Christians have been externally conformed to the rules instead of internally transformed by the gospel.

A Pure Heart Changes Your Desires

When You said, "Seek My face," my heart said to You, "Your face, LORD, I will seek."

—Psalm 27:8

Delight yourself also in the LORD, and He shall give you the desires of your heart.

—Psalm 37:4

Third, the pure heart is confirmed by a genuine change in what you want. When you develop a pure heart, it will impact your desires. The new heart will bring about new appetites. Whereas you used to long for the lust of the flesh, now you long for the purity of God. This doesn't mean you won't stumble and fall. On occasion, you may succumb to old desires. But the new heart will regain control, because its driving passion is to love and please God.

The Evidence of Redemption

King David was called a "man after God's own heart" (Acts 13:22). Yet he sinned mightily. One of the most famous stories tells of how he had an affair with a married woman and then sent her husband to die in battle. It's pretty amazing to see David's soul-level repentance.

Have mercy upon me, O God, according to Your lovingkindness; according to the multitude of Your tender mercies, blot out my transgressions. Wash me thoroughly from my iniquity, and cleanse me from my sin. For I acknowledge my transgressions, and my sin is always before me.

—Psalm 51:1-3

Through this story in the Old Testament and the story of the prostitute who anointed Jesus' feet with oil in the New Testament (Luke 7:46), we can understand that God values repentance and is quick to offer forgiveness to purify our hearts and to claim us as His own.

No matter where David went or what he did, he could never get away from the fact that his heart belonged to God. His first concern after committing adultery and sin was that his "inward parts" would be cleansed (Psalm 51:6). He wanted to have the integrity of his heart restored. The Pharisees may have never sinned the way David had, but they missed the most important issue: they didn't have pure hearts before God.

Jesus favors the prostitute who comes to Him with her whole heart over the self-righteous legalist who will not give Him his heart. Christ wants the pure, unmixed, undivided, genuine, holy heart.

Such a heart is received by faith. It's implanted by the Holy Spirit. And it's confirmed by a real, noticeable change in your desires.

WORKBOOK

Chapter Five Questions

Question: What words would you use to describe a pure heart? Why is it possible for Christians to have pure hearts?

_____

_____

_____

_____

_____

_____

_____

_____

_____

_____

_____

Question: What does it mean that humans have a three-fold nature? What are these three natures, and how does the Bible direct us to manage each one?

_____

_____

_____

_____

_____

_____

_____

_____

_____

_____

_____

Question: How do we obtain a pure heart? What evidence can we look for to confirm that our hearts are being purified?

_____

_____

_____

_____

_____

Action: Incorporating suggestions from this chapter, write out a list of ways in which God works to transform our souls. Choose one to focus on this week, and record how God uses it to continue to transform you.

Journal: Meditate on 2 Corinthians 5:17 and follow the STAR journal method. What does it mean to be a new creation in Christ?

Chapter Five Notes

_____

_____

_____

_____

_____

_____

_____

_____

_____

_____

_____

_____

_____

_____

_____

_____

_____

_____

_____

CHAPTER SIX

Renew Your Mind

Grace and peace be multiplied to you in the knowledge of God and of Jesus our Lord, as His divine power has given to us all things that pertain to life and godliness, through the knowledge of Him who called us by glory and virtue, by which have been given to us exceedingly great and precious promises, that through these you may be partakers of the divine nature, having escaped the corruption that is in the world through lust.

For he who lacks these things is shortsighted, even to blindness, and has forgotten that he was cleansed from his old sins.

—2 Peter 1:2–4, 9

The scripture above affirms the change of nature that occurs when we become born again. It affirms that we have been given promises, His divine nature, and a way of escape from corruption. We know that God transforms our hearts, but where does that leave our souls and bodies?

Verse 9 hammers this home. It says that if you lack this knowledge, you are shortsighted, blind, and have forgotten the past from which you were saved. If you have forgotten your past, then you need to be reminded here. You must choose whether or not you will partake of the divine nature.

This is such a powerful thought for this chapter. Just because you are born again, that does not automatically mean you will walk in all the benefits from God. We have laid a good foundation in this book that we must apprehend these promises in faith. We must renew our minds from old nature thinking to new nature thinking. You have a choice and a part to play in living out your identity in Christ.

We are spirit beings living in a physical world. How do we live according to the Spirit? When you can see the separation between spirit, soul, and body, you can deal with each as God instructs.

As we look at the following topic, I want you to notice how the authors of the biblical texts put importance on the will of man choosing to do or not to do certain parts of sanctification. God gives us the choice of obedience over and over again in Scripture. When we choose to obey, we reap the benefits of the promise. When we choose to rebel, we reap the consequences and lack of the benefits (Galatians 6:7–9).

Remember that God's love is without condition. God's love does not waver based on our choices of obedience or disobedience. Remember that you cannot be any more righteous than you are right now. God's imputed righteousness to you is not based on your behavior but His finished work. However, God's promises are very much conditional, and I think this is a good point to note as we study this chapter on some areas of responsibility in our sanctification. As you learn to walk in your identity in Christ, you will see fruits of your transformed life like obedience and holiness. We will explore this in later chapters.

> Therefore, since Christ suffered for us in the flesh, arm yourselves also with the same mind, for he who has suffered in the flesh has ceased from sin, that he no longer should live the rest of his time in the flesh for the lusts of men, but for the will of God. For we have spent enough of our past lifetime in doing the will of the Gentiles—when we walked in lewdness, lusts, drunkenness, revelries, drinking parties, and abominable idolatries.
> —1 Peter 4:1-3

Here is a clear distinction between the way we used to be outside of Christ and our new identity in Christ. Peter tells you to arm yourself. This is an offensive posture that says you are ready to do battle with any knowledge that is contrary to what God's Word says. If you are going to abide in your identity with Christ, it will take a militant posture toward anything that would try to get in the way, including your flesh and your unrenewed mind.

An Act of the Will

> Do not love the world or the things in the world. If anyone loves the world, the love of the Father is not in him. For all that is in the world—the lust of the flesh, the lust of the eyes, and the pride of life—is not of the Father but is of the world. And the world is passing away, and the lust of it; but he who does the will of God abides forever.

—*1 John 2:15-17*

Once again, you have a choice to love the things of the world or the things of the Father. If you do not renew your mind from the things of the world, you are doomed to live in the lust that is in the world. This will stunt and cripple your new identity in Christ.

The renewal of your mind is an act of your will. There are no magic answers to this. Renewal comes down to you making the choice to do things differently. It simply consists of you learning to live in your new identity in Christ and actively replacing the knowledge of your old thinking with the knowledge of God.

> *I beseech you therefore, brethren, by the mercies of God, that you present your bodies a living sacrifice, holy, acceptable to God, which is your reasonable service. And do not be conformed to this world, but be transformed by the renewing of your mind, that you may prove what is that good and acceptable and perfect will of God.*
> —**Romans 12:1-2**

The importance of Christians working hard to renew their minds is clear in this passage from Paul. He is begging Christians to take action, to take control, and to work toward renewal. He is saying that you are responsible to crucify your flesh and renew your mind. This sacrifice of the flesh is pleasing and worship to God. This renewing of your mind allows you to prove between what is of God and what is not. I don't know of anyone who would say that they don't want to know what God's will is for their life. As a matter of fact, as a pastor in a local biblical community, this is one of the most asked about questions. People are consistently looking to know what God's will is for their lives. Renewing your mind to what the Bible says about your identity will give you discernment in this.

> For the weapons of our warfare are not carnal but mighty in God for pulling down strongholds, casting down arguments and every high thing that exalts itself against the knowledge of God, bringing every thought into captivity to the obedience of Christ, and being ready to punish all disobedience when your obedience is fulfilled.
> —*2 Corinthians 10:4–6*

Here is another great example of the seriousness that is placed on this topic. If Christians could invest these truths into their lives, we would see a much more victorious church. This clearly states that we must arrest every argument and thought that is contrary to the knowledge of God. I think many Christians are carnal today, not because they are defeated by the enemy but because they simply do not walk in obedience to these truths.

Turning Our Minds from the World

While God wants us to strive for renewal, the truth is that we have many carnal Christians because we are distracted by worldly things, creating apathy to the truth of God. We do not give time to digest and walk out these clear instructions in Scripture, and so we don't benefit from the life that is within them. You can blame the devil, sin, or your busy lifestyle all day long. However, you are the only person whom God expects to do something about what He has given you as a son or daughter of His.

A simple example of this is the massive amount of unbiblical "food" we feed our souls on a weekly basis. We fill our minds and indulge our flesh in so many earthly, worldly things. On the flipside, we might journal once a week, shoot up a prayer around mealtime, visit a church service on Sunday, and expect our spirit to be fed well. I heard someone say years ago that most Christians feed their bodies three meals a day, and yet they give their spirits one cold snack a week. If you lived like this in nature, your body would not be healthy, and yet we do this all the time with our spirits and our souls. We have not renewed our minds and crucified our flesh, so what dominates us is our unrenewed minds and our carnal fleshly desires. Our redeemed spirit is crying out to lead us to Him and be fed, but it is overshadowed by worldly distractions.

You may think about the amount of work that it would take to consistently bring every thought into alignment with God's truth while also removing arguments. You are correct. This is why it is called discipleship and the fight of faith. Abiding in your identity is not a spectator sport. You must be engaged in this battle to walk in the fullness of your identity in Christ.

Another side to this is the massive amount of biblical knowledge that some Christians hold in their heads. We consume large quantities of sermons, books, podcasts, and so on. It's not a lack of knowledge that is causing this person's spiritual immaturity, but a lack of walking in what they know.

I have known people who are very disciplined and read through the Bible every year; they read multiple devotions a day, take notes on Sunday sermons, and could echo the Word of God right back to you. However, many of these same people have never appropriated or walked in the knowledge they have, and so it does not do them any good. It's like eating a hundred hot dogs at a contest and then assuming that will fill you up for the week. There is no way your body could digest that amount of food. Your body would reject it.

I have heard scholars discuss how cramming a large amount of information in your head once a week is not the best way to learn a new language. This will get you some understanding, but it will not sustain the learning process in the long term. They typically suggest doing smaller bits of study on a daily basis, which produces a stronger, more comprehensive understanding of the new language.

Simply put, the greatest measurement of you abiding in your identity in Christ is life transformation. As we have seen throughout this book, you can have many outward works that amount to simple religious duty and fall short of transformation. A disciple experiences continual transformation as they abide in Christ and mature in Him. The Lord gave me a simple way to understand and apply a process of transformation and renewal of my mind concepts. It involves three words that revolutionized my journey: Revelation, Application, Transformation. Before you can get to transformation, you must have a revelation from God. In God's blueprint for your life you must have a revelation of who God is, who you are in relation to Him, what God desires for you and has called you to do.

Revelation is a revealed, striking disclosure, especially something not realized before. So, it goes beyond simple knowledge and intellectual understanding. Revelation is a divinely spoken and imparted word from God directly to you. My definition of revelation is the ability to get from God directly what He has for your life and season and get it out on the table so that you can examine it, understand it, learn it, and walk in it.

After revelation comes application. Some people get a revelation of God's Word and expect that to transform them but they never apply the revelation to their lives and don't get to the transformation. This can be very confusing but it's really not. Others will come into a church environment and understand what is required from them from a mental assent perspective but it's not revelation to them. It is simply intellectual knowledge and it will not transform their life. They immediately start trying to religiously and dutifully apply this knowledge and expect transformation. There is the huge missing piece of revelation from God. As you abide in Christ, this revelation comes from Him by the power of the Holy Spirit initiating the direct words of God for your specific life and situation.

A Better Option

For indeed the gospel was preached to us as well as to them; but the word which they heard did not profit them, not being mixed with faith in those who heard it.

Are you starting to see the "abiding in identity" life-style? It's not about a onetime decision, a once-a-week church service, a once-a-year resolution. It's about daily abiding in intimacy with Christ. It's about letting your redeemed spirit dominate and be fed by the words of eternal life. It's about implementing the Word of God into your life and renewing your mind from the ways of sin, lust, and worldliness to the ways of God (Romans 12:2). It's about crucifying your flesh and letting your true identity dominate your life (Colossians 3:5).

I see people who are so distracted at all the things this life has to offer that they never appropriate and abide in their true identity. They have excuses as to why this is, but God holds each one of us responsible for our own spiritual journeys. It takes an act of your will to obey these truths.

I have noticed something in my discipleship journey with Christ over the past few years that has had a huge impact in my life. There are not a lot of horizontal things that catch my attention and draw me away from my intimacy with Christ. Many years ago, I could not say that. As I have matured in my walk with Christ, I have become totally devoted to my King, and I also have those whom I am leading as a fruit of my fellowship with my King. After I invest in all of these things, there is not a lot of time or energy left to spend on earthly, horizontal things that do not matter in light of eternity. I don't miss those things at all. I find such great joy in my intimacy with Christ that I am fulfilled.

The way to overcome sin is not by stirring up our will-power to say no—it's by stirring up our hearts to say yes to the all-satisfying joy of knowing Christ.[19]

—**C.S. Lewis**

Running toward the Prize

Do you not know that those who run in a race all run, but one receives the prize? Run in such a way that you may obtain it. And everyone who competes for the prize is temperate in all things. Now they do it to obtain a perishable crown, but we for an imperishable crown. Therefore I run thus: not with uncertainty. Thus, I fight: not as one who beats the air. But I discipline my body and bring it into subjection, lest, when I have preached to others, I myself should become disqualified.

—*1 Corinthians 9:24–27*

Paul has a lot to say on this topic in the Epistles, and he uses his own journey with Christ to back up these points. In the verse above, he once again lays out the idea that salvation, discipleship, and intimacy with Christ is not a onetime decision, but a series of decisions in walking by faith. This race he describes is a process. I want to call out a couple of points from these verses.

He encourages us to run in such a way that we may obtain "the prize." This prize is not a destination, but a Person. The prize is Christ. We are called to abide in Christ in intimacy and let Him define our lives. He is cautioning us to race in such a way that will keep us focused on what is most important.

He uses the word *temperate* to describe someone who is competing well. This word is *egkrateuomai*, which means to exercise self-control, or to have self-control. This word comes from the word *egkratēs*, which means "strong, master of, self-controlled."[20]

These words are not ambiguous or uncertain. Paul is clearly continuing this thought that the walk of faith is a fight, a battle, an all-out war. Not a physical war. The physical man is supposed to already be crucified. The war takes place in the realm of the mind. The war is renewing the mind to the Word of God and allowing the redeemed spirit to dominate (Romans 12:2).

Paul continues to describe this battle as one with confidence. He is not distracted or confused on what this war is all about. He said he has certainty that leads to definitive action (1 Corinthians 9:26–27). I think this is such an important point. If we go back the very premise of this book, you can see that righteousness is such an important concept to grasp. If you are uncertain of your identity and your position with Christ, you will never do battle with certainty. There will always be a hesitancy and insecurity because you will be basing your actions on a loose, unsecured foundation.

I hope you are seeing the power of this topic and why I think it is the most misunderstood topic in the body of Christ today. If you don't get your identity correct, you will never battle well, and you will not walk in the fullness of all God has for you. You will then blame so many things that are not to blame. Christ has given this gift and responsibility to you.

What things in your life are distracting you from walking in your identity with Christ?

I find then a law, that evil is present with me, the one who wills to do good. For I delight in the law of God according to the inward man. But I see another law in my members, warring against the law of my mind, and bringing me into captivity to the law of sin which is in my members. O wretched man that I am! Who will deliver me from this body of death? I thank God—through Jesus Christ our Lord! So then, with the mind I myself serve the law of God, but with the flesh the law of sin.
—Romans 7:21-25

Walking in the Spirit

Paul describes the battle that goes on between the inward man, the mind, and the law of sin in his members. This is a great example of navigating our human triune nature, the body, soul, and heart God has given to you. Can you see this battle in the verses above? Paul said his inward man, or his spirit being, delights in the Law of God. This is how you should be, as well. Your redeemed heart is always longing for the Law of God. He goes on to say that it is his members, or his flesh, warring against the law of his mind and captivating him into sin. He declares his flesh as being wretched and full of death. His plea is one of desiring freedom. He finishes with the declaration that Christ, His Lord, is the hope. He says that his flesh will continue to be fleshly, but with his mind, he determines to serve God.

He continues this in chapter 8 by breaking down what this deliverance looks like. I want you to take note of the verses ahead here. There is so much power and so many key elements to abiding in your identity here, along with the part a renewed mind plays in that.

There is therefore now no condemnation to those who are in Christ Jesus, who do not walk according to the flesh, but according to the Spirit. For the law of the Spirit of life in Christ Jesus has made me free from the law of sin and death. For what the law could not do in that it was weak through the flesh, God did by sending His own Son in the likeness of sinful flesh, on account of sin: He condemned sin in the flesh, that the righteous requirement of the law might be fulfilled in us who do not walk according to the flesh but according to the Spirit. For those who live according to the flesh set their minds on the things of the flesh, but those who live according to the Spirit, the things of the Spirit. For to be carnally minded is death, but to be spiritually minded is life and peace. Because the carnal mind is enmity against God; for it is not subject to the law of God, nor indeed can be. So then, those who are in the flesh cannot please God. But you are not in the flesh but in the Spirit, if indeed the Spirit of God dwells in you. Now if anyone does not have the Spirit of Christ, he is not His. And if Christ is in you, the body is dead because of sin, but the Spirit is life because of righteousness. But if the Spirit of Him who raised Jesus from the dead dwells in you, He who raised Christ from the dead will also give life to your mortal bodies through His Spirit who dwells in you. Therefore, brethren, we are debtors—not to the flesh, to live according to the flesh. For if you live according to the flesh you will die; but if by the Spirit you put to death the deeds of the body, you will live. For as many as are led by the Spirit of God, these are sons of God. For you did not receive the spirit of bondage again to fear, but you received the Spirit of adoption by whom we cry out, "Abba, Father." The Spirit Himself bears witness with our spirit that we are children of God, and if children, then heirs—heirs of God and joint heirs with Christ, if indeed we suffer with Him, that we may also be glorified together.

—Romans 8:1–17

Here is some insight on this passage to help it come alive for you:

- There is not any condemnation for you if you choose to walk in the Spirit and not the flesh. This is another example of the willful choice you have to walk in.

- Those who live according to the flesh set their minds on the things of the flesh.

- Those who live according to the Spirit set their minds on the things of the Spirit. Wow! What a powerful affirmation for us to renew our minds. You have the authority and power to renew your mind or to set it on fleshly, carnal things.

- To be carnally minded is death, but being spirit-minded is life and peace. If you will simply learn to renew your mind to your new identity in Christ, it will bring you life and peace.

- The carnal mind is at enmity with God. This means that you are in direct opposition to how God thinks. You are hostile, have hatred toward, have ill will toward, have animosity and antagonism toward God's words. This means that your mind and the thoughts you think are enemies of God. Wow, that is strong language. You are not subject to the Law of God, nor can you be. Your fruits are displeasing to God. You must learn to renew your mind to think like

God does and not after your flesh or worldly mindsets.

- If you are born again, you should live in the Spirit and experience the life of Christ because of your righteousness. You get to choose.

- This renewed mind accepts the spirit of adoption by God and cries out to Abba Father. The Holy Spirit bears witness with your spirit that you are a child of God. Your inner person knows your true identity. It's time to allow that to dominate the rest of your being. It is time to renew your mind to what your spirit knows.

- This renewed mind understands that you are not only a child of God, but an heir. You have been given a heritage from God. It's time to start walking in that and identifying as such.

Colossians 3:1–2 also focuses on our new identity and what that means for us.

If then you were raised with Christ, seek those things which are above, where Christ is, sitting at the right hand of God. Set your mind on things above, not on things on the earth.

Have you been raised with Christ? Are you His child? Then are you seeking His purpose, His things? Are you setting your mind and affections on Christ-knowledge or on earthly things? Do you see your perspective is at the right hand of God? This knowledge will change your life.

Choosing to Accept Your Identity

At this point in this book, there is no denying the clear and intentional identity in which we are called to live. You must simply accept this or reject it. Neither is a onetime decision but a daily discipline requiring you to abide in your identity because of whose you are. Being led by the Holy Spirit to your spirit is not an emotion but a knowing, and it usually doesn't feel good to align with your flesh or your unrenewed mind.

> *And I, brethren, could not speak to you as to spiritual people but as to carnal, as to babes in Christ. I fed you with milk and not with solid food; for until now you were not able to receive it, and even now you are still not able; for you are still carnal. For where there are envy, strife, and divisions among you, are you not carnal and behaving like mere men?*
> **—1 Corinthians 3:1–3**

Carnal Christians pursue milk instead of meat. This leaves you malnourished and unable to grow into all that God has for you. This leaves you living in the works of the flesh instead of the fruits of the Spirit. Mature believers are not the ones who have all the knowledge but the ones who accept by faith to walk in the knowledge they do have. Mature believers abide in their identity in Christ.

> *Now if anyone builds on this foundation with gold, silver, precious stones, wood, hay, straw, each one's work will*

become clear; for the Day will declare it, because it will be revealed by fire; and the fire will test each one's work, of what sort it is. If anyone's work which he has built on it endures, he will receive a reward. If anyone's work is burned, he will suffer loss; but he himself will be saved, yet so as through fire. Do you not know that you are the temple of God and that the Spirit of God dwells in you? If anyone defiles the temple of God, God will destroy him. For the temple of God is holy, which temple you are.
—1 Corinthians 3:12–17

How you build will become evident. If you invest in earthly, fleshly things, it will be exposed when God requires an account of your life. Don't be one who lives in carnality and does not abide in your true identity, and then is exposed for what you are in that day. Be someone who abides in Christ. Be a believer who fights the good fight of faith. Fight to renew your mind and allow your inner person to lead you. Fight to crucify your flesh and put it under complete control.

For though by this time you ought to be teachers, you need someone to teach you again the first principles of the oracles of God; and you have come to need milk and not solid food. For everyone who partakes only of milk is unskilled in the word of righteousness, for he is a babe. But solid food belongs to those who are of full age, that is, those who by reason of use have their senses exercised to discern both good and evil.
—Hebrews 5:12–14

The word "senses" here is *aistheterion*, and it means an "organ of perception, judgment, senses." This word comes from the word *aisthanomai*, which means, "to apprehend by the senses, perceive."[21]

In the context of this verse, we see that we are called to train our mental and soulish senses to think and act in response to the Word of God. You are now a partaker of the divine nature of God (2 Peter 1:4). This is exercise and discipline. It does not happen simply because you got saved. You must allow your re-created spirit to dominate the rest of your being. You must begin to think like God defines you in His Word. You must begin to renew your mind and think according to your new identity.

A New Approach

This new life and identity will be contrary to the way you have lived your entire life before Christ. This will take discipline and intentionality to live in. This is not a one-time decision. You must determine to live in the Spirit every day, all day. That is why this is called abiding in your identity. You must continue to remain here. The minute you are pulled aside to another identity or even driven by a fleshly lust, you start to live in an alternate identity to who you are in Christ.

And you, who once were alienated and enemies in your mind by wicked works, yet now He has reconciled in the body of His flesh through death, to present you holy, and blameless, and above reproach in His sight—if indeed you continue in the faith, grounded and steadfast, and are not moved away from the hope of the gospel which you heard, which was preached to every creature under heaven, of which I, Paul, became a minister.

—Colossians 1:21–23

This verse reminds you that you once were alienated and an enemy in your mind. I love the contrast to how you were after you were reconciled. Now you are presented by Christ as blameless, holy, and above reproach in His sight. This comes with an "if," however. If you continue in the faith, grounded, steadfast, and not moving away from the gospel, you are blameless. Like I mentioned earlier, God's love is without condition, but His promises are very conditional.

> Blessed is the man who endures temptation; for when he has been approved, he will receive the crown of life which the Lord has promised to those who love Him. Let no one say when he is tempted, "I am tempted by God"; for God cannot be tempted by evil, nor does He Himself tempt anyone. But each one is tempted when he is drawn away by his own desires and enticed. Then, when desire has conceived, it gives birth to sin; and sin, when it is full-grown, brings forth death.
>
> Do not be deceived, my beloved brethren. Every good gift and every perfect gift is from above, and comes down from the Father of lights, with whom there is no variation or shadow of turning. Of His own will He brought us forth by the word of truth, that we might be a kind of firstfruits of His creatures.
>
> —James 1:12–18

The book of James has so many powerful truths for us as believers. Here in chapter 1 we see that we are cautioned to be aware of temptation. I was taught that temptation comes from the devil and that he is the great deceiver. This is true, and the Scriptures tell us not to be ignorant of his devices (2 Corinthians 2:11). However, here in James we see another truth that deals with temptation, and it helps support the power of a renewed mind.

James tells us that when we are tempted, we are not to blame God, because God does not tempt us to sin. God will test us, but He does not tempt us. These are very different. Temptation is an enticement to sin and God does not do that. Testing is a proving or proof of what is inside of you. James says that each one of us is tempted when we are drawn away by our own desires and enticed. This is a key point about abiding in your identity. If your mind is not renewed to God's Word, your desires will not be His. And those desires will ultimately end up drawing you away and enticing you. This desire then conceives and gives birth to sin, and sin, when it is full grown, produces death (James 1:15). Do you see the subtlety of the damage that an unrenewed mind can do to your identity in Christ?

When you walk outside of a renewed mind, you have no one to blame but yourself for the sin that you are enticed into. On the flipside, when you understand this principle of renewing your mind with the Word of God, you will see a major shift in your affections, desires, and ability to resist temptation and sinful desires. These truths are not difficult to understand, but they will take a journey of intimacy with Christ to walk in.

How to Handle Extreme Emotion

So then, my beloved brethren, let every man be swift to hear, slow to speak, slow to wrath; for the wrath of man does not produce the righteousness of God.

—James 1:19–20

The next verses in this chapter hammer home the point of the renewal of the mind. In verses 19–20, we see the terms "slow to wrath" and the "wrath of man." I want to focus in on this word *wrath*. I have been taught as most Christians have that this word refers to anger and rage. While that is one of the definitions of this word, it also has other meanings.

I was studying this one day and thought how these two verses did not seem to fit into the context of the rest of the chapter. The chapter is talking about temptation, and then it makes a hard turn to caution us about anger? This didn't add up to me. Anger is not even being talked about. Even verses 21 through the end of the chapter are addressing the cleansing of the soul by being doers of the word and not just hearers. (I'll speak to that in a moment.)

As I began to study this word *wrath*, I saw another Greek meaning that made much more sense in the context of the chapter.

James Strong's *Concordance and Bible Dictionary* defines this instance of *wrath* as *orge*, "a desire (as a reaching forth or excitement of the mind) ... violent passion ... anger, indignation, vengeance, wrath."[22] It comes from the primary word *oregō*, which describes a stretching out, reaching after, or yearning for something—that is, longing or desire.[23]

If we put these definitions together, we can clearly pull out the intended meaning: renewing our mind in our desires. James is telling us to be slow in what we grasp and long for, wish and want, and aspire. He is cautioning us to be slow to pursue our desires or affections with excitement. This is such powerful truth. He says the wrath of man, passion of man, the reaching after, yearning for, desire, longing, and aspiring of man, does not produce the righteousness of God.

We must first filter our passions and desires through the grid of God's Word and the power of the Holy Spirit.

This continues the narrative of abiding in your identity. Only God can define righteousness and your identity in Him. Why would you come to Him for salvation and then pursue your own wrath, passions, desires, longings, and so on? This makes no sense.

However, if you have never known or been taught that you have a part to play in your ongoing sanctification and abiding in your identity, then you would not know to do anything different.

You are going to be tempted. Temptation from the enemy or your own desires is not sinful. It's when you are quick to act upon those temptations with passion and excitement and not allow your spirit and renewed mind to filter these desires that sin enters in.

You have the will to choose how you will react or act with the desires and temptations that arise. You can have victory by living out of your redeemed heart and your renewed mind. Or you can quickly pursue whatever comes your way without the governance of the Holy Spirit and be enticed into sin, sometimes grievous sin unto death. It is your choice and responsibility.

James goes on to say that we are not to be deceived by what gifts, passions, desires, or temptations are presented to us. God does not change, and His gifts are good and perfect (James 1:17). Of His own will He brought us forth by the word of truth (James 1:18). Do you anchor your thoughts, affections, meditations, and passions on this, or on your own desires and temptations?

What is God trying to get across here? The next verses in this sequence give you affirmation on how to do this.

> *Therefore lay aside all filthiness and overflow of wickedness, and receive with meekness the implanted word, which is able to save your souls. But be doers of the word, and not hearers only, deceiving yourselves. For if anyone is a hearer of the word and not a doer, he is like a man observing his natural face in a mirror; for he observes himself, goes away, and immediately forgets what kind of man he was. But he who looks into the perfect law of liberty and continues in it, and is not a forgetful hearer but a doer of the work, this one will be blessed in what he does.*
> —*James 1:21–25*

Once again, you see that He tells you to do something to walk in these truths. He tells you what to lay aside and what to invest in and obey. A redeemed heart and a renewed mind will lay aside sinful things and be a doer of the Word, not just a hearer, like most Christians are today. Not just a milk drinker, but a meat eater. Not a babe in Christ, but a fully formed disciple. Not just an imitator, but a teacher (Hebrews 5:12–14). You can hear and be around what God is doing, but you must choose to be a doer of His Word to see any impact on your life.

> *For the word of God is living and powerful, and sharper than any two-edged sword, piercing even to the division of*

soul and spirit, and of joints and marrow, and is a discerner of the thoughts and intents of the heart.
—Hebrews 4:12

You must learn to love the Word of God. It is this that will feed your spirit and nurture your soul. The Word of God is the only thing that has the power to discern among your triune nature. The God kind of faith can only be appropriated where God's will is known. We know that God's Word is His will and that faith comes from the Word.

He Has Made the Way

Are you seeing a pattern here? Are you building up confidence to walk in faith in your identity?

If you are trying to have faith in a feeling or something someone said, it will not produce any Kingdom fruit. Your faith must be in the Word of God. The renewing of your mind is what the Scriptures call the washing of the Word (Romans 12:2; Ephesians 5:26). Jesus said in John 15:3 that we are already clean because of His Word. However, our minds must be washed and renewed on a continual basis to have clear discernment on what His will is.

What are some practical things that you can do to crucify your flesh, renew your mind, and allow your redeemed spirit to dominate?

WORKBOOK

Chapter Six Questions

Question: "God's love is without conditions.... God's promises are very much conditional." What are some examples of this principle from Scripture?

_____

_____

_____

_____

_____

_____

_____

_____

_____

_____

_____

Question: What does it mean—both spiritually and practically—to renew your mind? How can you do this on a daily, ongoing basis?

_____

_____

_____

_____

_____

_____

_____

_____

_____

_____

_____

Question: What is the battleground in the fight of faith? What distractions keep you from victoriously living in your identity in Christ? Is your mind more set on the eternal or the temporal—and how can a person have their mind set on heavenly things while still taking care of earthly responsibilities?

_____

_____

_____

_____

_____

_____

_____

_____

_____

_____

_____

_____

Action: Where are you setting your mind? Make a list of things that distract and keep you from renewing your mind and a list of things that help you in the battle for the mind. Note over the course of the next week how much time you are giving to each major influence.

_____

_____

_____

_____

_____

_____

_____

_____

_____

_____

_____

_____

Journal: Meditate on James 1:12–25 and follow the STAR journal process. Ask God to give you His perspective and control over your passions and desires.

Chapter Six Notes

_____

_____

_____

_____

_____

_____

_____

_____

_____

_____

_____

_____

_____

_____

_____

_____

_____

_____

_____

_____

_____

_____

CHAPTER SEVEN

I Am the Righteousness of God in Christ

Years ago, I was heading to a meeting to meet a friend and ministry mentor. After I checked in at the front desk, I heard someone yell from the top of the stairs. I looked up and greeted him. His next words opened up a character issue for me that would begin a journey of identity restoration. He yelled down, "Nate Sweeney, you mighty man of courage." When he said that, something inside of me felt weird and I immediately looked down. Something did not sit right with me in that moment. When I went up the stairs, he questioned me about what had happened. We talked about how when I was addressed as a man of courage, something in me felt shameful and I did not see myself that way. For some reason, I did not identify that way, but I felt discouraged and unworthy. That started a season of digging into the Word and finding out why I felt this way. I eventually found the root cause and found healing from that wound. I no longer struggle with that specific part of my identity in Christ.

I share this story to remind you that discipleship is a journey that will take you the rest of your life. There is no magic formula you can use that will make you grow instantly. These principles in this book are ones that must be applied and lived out for them to have an effect in your life. I want you to start seeing yourself as God sees you and not how others do or Satan does. There are so many things in today's climate that are directly assaulting your identity in Christ. Your enemy wants you to be confused and distant from the true identity in Christ. He will assault you with false images, comparison, lust of the eyes, temptation into sin, shame, guilt, condemnation, and anything else to draw you away from who you are in Christ.

Your intimate, abiding relationship with Christ should affect every other area of your life. Too many Christians allow things outside of Christ and His Word to define their identity, purpose, and soul. This should not be so. You must get the revelation of who you are in Christ into your inner person, renew your mind with what God says about you, and crucify the flesh and old person that would try and keep you bound in unrighteousness.

Replacing your current identity by abiding in your identity in Christ is the key to living in righteousness. To self-identify as anything short of what God has given to you in His Word is living in the lies that the enemy uses to keep you in bondage.

Here are some truths that may reveal to you other things that might be competing for your identity and abiding in righteousness:

- If you identify more with your denominational leaning or religious group than who you are in Christ, then you are not abiding in your identity in Christ.

- If you identify more with how people see you or describe you based on your past circumstances, sinful tendencies, or any other horizontal-level measurement than who you are in Christ, you are not abiding in your identity in Christ.

- If you identify more with your role, last name, occupation, or marital status than who you are in Christ, you are not abiding in your identity in Christ.

- If you identify with your gifts or talents more than who you are in Christ, you are not abiding in your identity in Christ.

- If you identify more with your sexuality, gender, or social status than who you are as a son or daughter of God, you are not abiding in your identity in Christ.

- If you identify more with your citizenship of the country you live in than your citizenship in heaven, you are not abiding in your identity in Christ.

- If you identify more with a political party, sports team, or hobby than who you are in Christ, you are not abiding in your identity in Christ.

- If you identify more with your race, socioeconomic status, or social justice reforming movements than who you are in Christ, you are not abiding in your identity in Christ.

- If you tolerate sin in your own life or the lives of others in the name of "love," then you are not abiding in your identity in Christ.

What is hindering you from abiding in righteousness? If you are not living in the righteousness of Christ, maybe you have not been crucified with Him (Galatians 2:20)? Maybe you relate more to your sin nature and not your new nature in Christ? Maybe you have a sin consciousness instead of a God consciousness? Maybe how you came to Christ has had a negative effect on how you live for Him? I pray this book offers some biblical insight into what it looks like when your identity is in Christ.

All of these conversations must be wrapped up in your abiding identity in Christ, not the other way around. You should not find your identity in anything on a horizontal level that has not first been filtered through who God says you are in Christ. When you abide in your identity in Christ, all of these other areas will align themselves under the authority of who you *are* in Christ.

Paul's Struggle with Identity

I have heard over and over, as far back as I can remember how the great apostle Paul, who wrote a large portion of the New Testament and had revelation experience and a direct visitation from Christ, struggled with his own identity. If there is no hope for this great church leader, where does this leave me? However, this is another prime example where people have misinterpreted Scripture to fit a narrative of unrighteousness. This infuriates me, because this type of unrenewed thinking leads people to neglect abiding in their true identity in Christ.

We have already looked at Romans 7 and 8 in the previous chapters on this point. We clearly saw that the struggle was not that Paul was living in an unworthy mindset, but he was laying out a pattern of managing the triune nature of humanity. Paul acknowledged that our flesh and mind will want the things of this world. But our heart—the thing that has been transformed—has the power to effect change over our whole being.

> *For if you live according to the flesh you will die; but if by the Spirit you put to death the deeds of the body, you will live.*
>
> **—Romans 8:13**

All of Romans 8:1–17 has Paul showing that God has given us clear directives on how to feed our spirit, renew our mind, and crucify the flesh.

Here is another place that I have heard used to affirm that even Paul saw himself as a worm and struggled with his identity in Christ.

> *This is a faithful saying and worthy of all acceptance, that Christ Jesus came into the world to save sinners, of whom I am chief.*
>
> **—1 Timothy 1:15**

Many say that this verse is Paul's admission that he was the commander and chief of sinners and the worst person who has ever lived. Some translations even add emphasis in the text to drive this point home. This is not only bad translating, it goes back to the half-truth conversation earlier in this book. A pure translation is created outside of feeling or belief. A skewed translation is created with the intent to lead the reader to a conclusion that may or may not be there.

The word *chief* used here is the Greek word *prōtos*.[24] The most common way this word was used was to mean "first in time, place, in any succession of things or of persons." It is found over 150 times in the New Testament with Paul using the term and this definition nearly thirty times. There is not any evidence in other passages that Paul used this word in any secondary meanings. So, the context of how he used this word was that he was saying he was in sequential order and not in a highest-to-lowest ranking. Make sense?

Paul clearly understood that he was a sinner, and he transparently shared his life story with us in the pages he wrote. However, he also recognized that God had redeemed and transformed him and that he was no longer a sinner saved by grace but a son of God and an heir with Christ (Romans 8:17). Paul's admission to sin was a part of his conversion and should be similarly recognized in all of us. After conversion, though, we should walk in our new identity. If you simply take verse 15 in the context of the rest of his letter to Timothy, he clearly was talking about his former identity versus his new one. He never said or even hinted that he was the worst sinner ever to live or that he was still in that state. He only showed that he was the first in a sequential order of many sinners whom God would redeem. The next verses even say that God was using Paul's story as a pattern for those who would believe for everlasting life. The rest of his writings show him abiding in righteousness, not a sinner bound to sin. Basically, he was saying that God did it in his life and He will do it many times over in others.

Why, then, has this been so widely misinterpreted? I would assume that it falls in line with a lot that we have seen in this book. It is impossible for a mind that has not been renewed in the Word of God to accept the righteousness of God and apply that to their life. This is a huge point of this chapter. We must know and appropriate our new identity in Christ so that we can live in its benefits.

False Humility

Speaking to the quote by Martin Luther at the beginning of chapter 1—"What greater rebellion, impiety, or insult to God can there be, than not to believe His promises?"[25]—I want to share some thoughts on false humility. Years ago, I used to have a hard time sharing my story and all that God had done and was doing in me. I used to think it was prideful to talk about how good God had been to me. I didn't want others feeling bad because God was blessing me if it didn't seem like He was doing the same for them. Even in my preaching, I would refrain from using much of my story or all of the wonderful things God had done, for fear of coming across as prideful or more spiritual than others. God began to show me how He wants me to use my story for His glory.

It is actually a false form of humility to keep to yourself what God has done. When we try too hard to appear humble, it can actually come across as annoying. It's not humble to downplay the bestowed righteousness from God. It's dishonoring to minimize His gift. As we have seen throughout this book, people honor transparency and authenticity. They can smell a fake a mile away. People want to hear how God delivered you from the depths of sin and from your bad choices. They need to be able to relate to your story. When you neglect to share this with others, you put off a certain aura that lacks authenticity. Your story should be saturated with humility, true humility, which knows that you didn't deliver, heal, or restore yourself. Only God can take credit for your story if you have walked with Him.

Obviously, this can be misused and turn into pride and arrogance. If your story talks more about you and your wild days of sin, and less about the glory of God, then maybe you should not share it with others. When your story is shared, it should always point to God and His purposes and workings in your life. It should never boast you up. Your story should offer hope in Christ to others.

Others need our stories to see a pattern of living in the righteousness of God. They need to know that what they are seeing is attainable. They can use your story as a point of faith to trust God and His Word. Here are a handful of scriptures that talk about us using our story for God's purposes.

And they overcame him by the blood of the Lamb and by the word of their testimony, and they did not love their lives to the death.

—Revelation 12:11

There are spiritual leaders in your life whom God has placed there as mentors, fathers, and mothers so that you would have a pattern to follow. These people should care for your soul and be a catalyst to help you to abide in your identity in Christ.

I do not write these things to shame you, but as my beloved children I warn you. For though you might have ten thousand instructors in Christ, yet you do not have many fathers; for in Christ Jesus I have begotten you through the gospel. Therefore I urge you, imitate me. For this reason I have sent Timothy to you, who is my beloved and faithful son in the Lord, who will remind you of my ways in Christ, as I teach everywhere in every church.

—1 Corinthians 4:14–17

Imitate me, just as I also imitate Christ.

—1 Corinthians 11:1

On the other end of the spectrum are those in your life for whom God has called you to be a spiritual leader and to encourage. You should be an example of Christ to help them abide in their identity in Him. If you walk as you are called, God will surround you with others into whom you can invest.

Let no one despise your youth, but be an example to the believers in word, in conduct, in love, in spirit, in faith, in purity.

—1 Timothy 4:12

Let us hold fast the confession of our hope without wavering, for He who promised is faithful. And let us consider one another in order to stir up love and good works, not forsaking the assembling of ourselves together, as is the manner of some, but exhorting one another, and so much the more as you see the Day approaching.

—Hebrews 10:23–25

Beyond the close personal relationships in which God will call you to invest, there are those in your sphere of influence whom God puts directly in your path. These are the ones to whom you get to simply reflect Christ's love and light. When you abide in your identity in Christ, you are attractive to the world and God will use you to express His love to them.

You are the light of the world. A city that is set on a hill cannot be hidden. Nor do they light a lamp and put it under a basket, but on a lampstand, and it gives light to all who are in the house. Let your light so shine before men, that they may see your good works and glorify your Father in heaven.

—Matthew 5:14–16

Therefore, if anyone is in Christ, he is a new creation; old things have passed away; behold, all things have become new. Now all things are of God, who has reconciled us to Himself through Jesus Christ, and has given us the ministry of reconciliation, that is, that God was in Christ reconciling the world to Himself, not imputing their trespasses to them, and has committed to us the word of reconciliation. Now then, we are ambassadors for Christ, as though God were pleading through us: we implore you on Christ's behalf, be reconciled to God. For He made Him who knew no sin to be sin for us, that we might become the righteousness of God in Him.

—2 Corinthians 5:17–21

Now thanks be to God who always leads us in triumph in Christ, and through us diffuses the fragrance of His knowledge in every place. For we are to God the fragrance of Christ among those who are being saved and among those who are perishing. To the one we are the aroma of death leading to death, and to the other the aroma of life leading to life. And who is sufficient for these things? For we are not, as so many, peddling the word of God; but as of sincerity, but as from God, we speak in the sight of God in Christ.

—2 Corinthians 2:14–17

The Story of Two Prodigals

In Luke 15:11–32, we are told the story of the prodigal son. At least this is what I was taught and even the heading in my Bible led me to believe that is what the parable is about. What I saw years ago, however, was that there were two prodigals in this story, and this understanding changed how I viewed much of Jesus' teaching in this passage.

The first son in this story left his father's home in search of prodigal living. The word *prodigal* is defined as "wasteful, reckless, or extravagant."[26] The son demanded his inheritance from his father and then proceeded to waste it in a sinful lifestyle. In the story, he came to a place of clarity and realized that even the servants in his father's house were living better than he was. He makes the statement that he is no longer worthy to be a son, and he is determined to grovel for his father's kindness. He hopes to be welcomed back as a hired servant or an employee. Just to be clear, we are all called to be servants of God. However, the type of "servant" the prodigal son was referring to here was a hired employee, or a slave. It is not the same as what we are called to be as children of God. We are all called to be servants as a fruit of our identity in Christ.

The prodigal son in the story followed through with his plan and went back to his father's house. He was planning to repent and ask to be allowed back into his father's kingdom—not as a son, but as a slave. Before he even got down the driveway, however, the father saw him and ran to him, had compassion for him, then fell on his neck and kissed him. The prodigal tried to give his rehearsed "I'm unrighteous" speech to his father, but the father would have nothing to do with it. The father immediately called for the total restoration of his son. He did not scold him or preach at him, but instead he offered him full familial restoration. This is the power of repentance and grace.

I meet so many Christians who feel the same way about their relationship with God as did this first prodigal. They have a sin consciousness that keeps them from accepting that they are a son or a daughter. They grovel in prayer and petitions to God, asking to be a hired employee in His kingdom, all the while missing how God the Father already sees them through His eyes. We need to appropriate, in faith, our identity in Christ. He did not do all He has done for us to merely be hired employees. We are sons and daughters. When you are bound up in a sin consciousness, you lose the boldness to live as He transformed you, and you settle for an unrighteous secondary role.

The second—less obvious—prodigal son is the one I can relate to well. This son never left his father's house. As far as I can tell, he fulfilled all the rules and regulations that were asked of a son. When he found out that his brother had come back and he saw his father's response, this second prodigal was indignant and refused to come in to celebrate. He did not have the heart of the father, but he lived with an unrighteous attitude. He pointed out to the father everything he had done for his father all these years and how horrible the first prodigal had treated his family. The second son had also been reckless with the benefits of being in his father's house. He lived under his father's roof, but he saw himself as a hired servant and not a son. The father was clear about his feelings: "Son, you are always with me, and all that I have is yours." However, this second prodigal did not see the father-son relationship that way. His relationship was based on his works. Everything was external and not internal to this second son. Even if you live in the Father's house, if you do not understand your identity in Him, you are a prodigal at heart and you will never find the joy of your salvation.

I remember years ago, before I got the revelation that I am sharing with you here, I lived with a sin consciousness and an unrighteous mindset. I used to complain that I had spent so many years in the church serving God, learning, and studying Scripture, but I didn't have the joy that some of these new believers had. I didn't have the revelation and spiritual hunger that some of these new believers enjoyed. I used to get so angry when people were able to walk through their sin and find grace and redemption because it was something I longed for, worked for, strived for, and yet didn't have. I know this sounds so twisted and backward, but it is where I was.

One day I realized that I was a religious, self-righteous, and unrighteous man. I came to Christ by grace through faith, but I was trying to earn my sanctification. It was still works-based, self-righteous living. I was a prodigal at heart because of my perceived unrighteousness and unworthiness. I did not understand my new identity in Christ, and so I was not able to walk in it. I was not able to celebrate the coming home of any other prodigals because it was a challenge and threat to my identity. I only related to God as a hired employee.

In my experience, the majority of people in the church today live this way as well. They live with a hired-employee and works-based righteousness. They live with a sin consciousness that puts a wedge between them and Father God. They don't realize the promises of God that are theirs in Christ, and therefore they never faithfully partake of them. This is the entire reason I have written this book.

I want to shed light on this deception and help people live in the Father's house as sons and daughters.

Hurts, Habits, and Hang-Ups

I asked earlier, what is hindering you from walking in your identity in Christ? This section may help shed light on many areas that you are allowing to get in the way. When you refuse to find healing from pain through the biblical process, you eventually find your identity in that sin, hurt, habit, or hang-up, and you become a victim. You can only be truly healed and delivered, and you will only find freedom from these things when you abide in your identity in Christ.

For you see your calling, brethren, that not many wise according to the flesh, not many mighty, not many noble, are called. But God has chosen the foolish things of the world to put to shame the wise, and God has chosen the weak things of the world to put to shame the things which are mighty; and the base things of the world and the things which are despised God has chosen, and the things which are not, to bring to nothing the things that are, that no flesh should glory in His presence. But of Him you are in Christ Jesus, who became for us wisdom from God—and righteousness and sanctification and redemption—that, as it is written, "He who glories, let him glory in the LORD."

And I, brethren, when I came to you, did not come with excellence of speech or of wisdom declaring to you the testimony of God. For I determined not to know anything among you except Jesus Christ and Him crucified. I was with you in weakness, in fear, and in much trembling. And my speech and my preaching were not with persuasive words of human wisdom, but in demonstration of the Spirit

and of power, that your faith should not be in the wisdom of men but in the power of God.
—1 Corinthians 1:26–2:5

Blessed be the God and Father of our Lord Jesus Christ, the Father of mercies and God of all comfort, who comforts us in all our tribulation, that we may be able to comfort those who are in any trouble, with the comfort with which we ourselves are comforted by God.
—2 Corinthians 1:3–4

Paul did not presume to be perfect or sinless. However, he did operate out of his identity in Christ as well as in total dependence. Second Corinthians 1 reminds us that God uses anyone who will allow Him to, no matter what excuses may be in the way. The rest of this chapter has been written to help you identify any hurts, habits, or hang-ups that may be hindering you from embracing your identity in Christ. God will use your story of suffering, tribulation, and restoration to assist others and bring Him glory.

Where do our character defects come from? Based on John Rosemond's *Parenting by the Book* and a section entitled "Postmodern Psychological Parenting,"[27] most believe our defects are a hybrid of three schools of psychological thought that are historically antagonistic to Christianity. While they are fundamentally wrong, it's important to see how these have played a part in leading people astray.

Freudian, Humanistic, and Behavioral Schools of Thought

From Sigmund Freud, the father of modern psychology, comes the *Freudian* principle of psychological determinism—the notion that human behavior is shaped by early childhood experiences. For example, negative toilet training experiences can cause later personality problems. So pretty much, as parents, we roam around terrified of making a wrong child-raising choice and scarring our children for life.

The *humanist* contribution consists of two propositions: 1) Children are fundamentally good, and 2) high self-esteem is a desirable attribute.

Finally, the *behavioral* school has contributed the idea that behavior modification works as well on human beings as it does on rats and dogs.

These three philosophies contradict the biblical point of view, and they also contradict common sense and social science research. Unfortunately, these viewpoints have become so embedded in collective thought that most people take them for granted, automatically classifying them as truth. Most people would be surprised to learn that not one of Freud's ideas has survived the test of scientific scrutiny. An article in *Newsweek* magazine called him "modern history's most debunked doctor."[28]

Parents and family environment (nurture) are a logical place where many try to assign blame for their later issues in life. You can look at most any study on any topic and walk away with the conclusion that environment is highly significant in how kids develop into later adults (abuse, religion, culture, social status, financial aspects being just a few that have been studied). I am not denying that point. However, this has become a major scapegoat of excuse for many adults today. We tend to try to affix blame on outside experience as to why we are the way we are.

Even though our experiences help to shape who we are, as sons and daughters of God we must learn to walk in our identity in Him and not based on what has happened to us. This is a difficult conversation for many who have had painful experiences in their past. I would never try to minimize anyone's pain or experiences. However, I have yet to find a pain or experience that was beyond the grace and mercy of a loving God, when people find their true identity in Him instead of in their past.

Here are some examples of how the past can become a crutch, no matter how bad or good our experiences have been:

"My parents had a horrible marriage, and my experience in this has led me to have a horrible marriage."

"My parents had a wonderful marriage; I simply cannot live up to their example, and so this is why my marriage is falling apart."

According to this line of thinking, there is never any way of breaking out of our past hurts. Instead of looking to the hope in Christ, we defer the responsibility and blame to others.

So, you can sit here today and derive a victim mentality as to why you are where you are today. Or you can immerse yourself in an intimate, abiding relationship with Christ and allow Him to transform your heart, which in turn will affect your choices, character, and destiny as you claim His promises. No matter what influences have shaped your life up until this point, your future is a product of your choices and not because you are a victim of your circumstances.

A true victim and self-righteous mentality is dangerous, because anything that gets in the way of you being in control or you being the center of attention sets you at war against them.

The real core issue is your sinful nature. We have replaced individual sin and depravity with institutional dysfunction or environment as being at fault for our issues. This leaves us without any personal responsibility. When you view yourself as a victim, you see your sin as something you need healing from instead of the core issue that it is. This all goes back to identity and what nature we are living in.

> *And you He made alive, who were dead in trespasses and sins, in which you once walked according to the course of this world, according to the prince of the power of the air, the spirit who now works in the sons of disobedience, among whom also we all once conducted ourselves in the lusts of our flesh, fulfilling the desires of the flesh and of the mind, and were by nature children of wrath, just as the others.*
> **—Ephesians 2:1–3**

The Bible clearly wants us to acknowledge our past, our hurts, our environment, the sins we have committed, and the sins that have been committed against us. The reason for this examination is to bring us to a place of repentance and grace. If we only acknowledge our problems through the grid of environment, we leave no room for what Jesus taught us in the Beatitudes about brokenness, repentance, mourning over sin, and so on. The core issue is your sinful nature.

All of your horizontal good works cannot balance out the scales of your sinful nature. All biblical transformation begins with proximity to Christ, and it opens the door to an intimate abiding relationship with Him. This is the Christ model. There is no program, class, or sermon series that can transform a person. Bringing people close to Christ allows the transformation process to take place.

If all the checks and balances were removed from your life, would you be able to regulate your nature and be a good person? Religion tries to address the physical and soulish problems in people, while Christ goes straight to the heart, knowing that a change of the heart will produce a change in the other two. Without inward conversion and transformation, there is no need to expect outward changes. You can be in church and not be saved. You can be spiritual but not have the indwelling of the Holy Spirit. You can love religion and your denomination but not love Christ. You can be a Christian and still live according to your old nature.

How many people have fallen in love with Jesus, but it ends there? There is no acknowledgment of sin, repentance, or lifestyle change. They admire Jesus like they do other good things, but not enough to make Him Lord of their life. How many people become a Christian but never walk in their full identity in Him? This topic is so vital to your health and for the health of the body of Christ.

Do you see yourself as the righteousness of God in Christ? Have you been able to identify any areas that get in the way of your identity in Christ?

WORKBOOK

Chapter Seven Questions

Question: What are some of the things Satan uses to keep people from their identity in Christ? What are some good relationships or associations from which a person might wrongly draw their identity instead of drawing it from Christ? Which have kept you personally from fully embracing the righteousness of Christ?

_____

_____

_____

_____

_____

_____

_____

_____

_____

_____

_____

Question: What is false humility? Is it prideful to use your own life as an example for others to follow? Why or why not?

_____

_____

_____

_____

_____

_____

_____

_____

_____

_____

_____

_____

Question: How were both sons in the parable prodigals? What was the difference? Which one do you identify with more? Do you see yourself as a hired servant or a beloved son or daughter?

_____

_____

_____

_____

_____

_____

_____

_____

_____

_____

_____

_____

Action: Make a bullet list of the major events of your life. From which ones do you draw a false identity? Are you carrying a victim mentality due to some of them? Which can be told to God's glory as a testimony of how He has redeemed and transformed you?

_____

_____

_____

_____

_____

_____

_____

_____

_____

_____

_____

_____

Journal: Meditate on the story of the Prodigal Son found in Luke 15:11–32. Use the STAR journal process. Ask God to reveal not only your heart but His as you study this parable.

Chapter Seven Notes

_____

_____

_____

_____

_____

_____

_____

_____

_____

_____

_____

_____

_____

_____

_____

_____

_____

_____

_____

_____

CHAPTER EIGHT

A Tale of Three Kingdoms

Life is hard.
It's not about you.
You are not in control.
You are going to die.[29]
    —Richard Rohr, Franciscan priest

To carry a cross means you are walking away and never
coming back.[30]
    —A. W. Tozer

When Christ calls a man, he bids him to come and die.[31]
    —Dietrich Bonhoeffer

A young woman had been pursuing righteousness.
More and more she was finding her identity in Christ.
While the experience was giving her clarity and communion with God as never before, she was struck by how deep
the process went. With tears in her eyes, she went to her
spiritual mentor. "Every day, God reveals to me a new

area that I have kept from Him. Every day I am reminded of how far I still have yet to go."

The elderly mentor embraced the woman. "I don't see it that way," she told the young believer. "Every day you are reminded exactly why you need to continue doing what you are doing!"

> *I have been crucified with Christ; it is no longer I who live, but Christ lives in me; and the life which I now live in the flesh I live by faith in the Son of God, who loved me and gave Himself for me.*
> *—Galatians 2:20*

This chapter may seem like a tough pill to swallow, but the life of a disciple is one of beautiful difficulty. If you are going to abide in your identity in Christ, it will confront all other forms of identity in which you have lived for so many years. There will be a tendency to fight what God is doing in you, as your old nature screams to stay alive and dominate the new you.

This chapter can also open you up for shame and disappointment inside you as you compare your life with the standard of Scripture. The point of this is not to shame or disappoint you, but merely to expose the false you and give you freedom to abide in who you are called to be in Christ. Satan himself is the author of condemnation. The truth of God's Word does not condemn you unless you reject it. The Word of God will bring conviction when you begin to understand that a change is needed in your life. When God exposes a false identity in your life, it is an act of His grace. He is giving you the opportunity to see the light and truth and make the necessary changes to walk in them.

Please allow the next chapters to be an encouragement to point you in the direction of your identity in Christ. We have already laid the strong foundation for your righteousness in Christ. If you will allow that foundation to take root in your life, then you can build upon it the way God intends.

First Kingdom: My Kingdom

Many in the church today are deceived by what they believe is their place in the body of Christ. Many have called upon Jesus to save them from hell, but they have not progressed past that point. They understand Jesus to be the One who saves them from things, gives them things, and blesses them with things. But there is no lifestyle of repentance, submission, discipline, or obedience.

These people think their life is about them and their kingdom. All roads in their kingdom lead to them. They only invite others in who will serve their kingdom desires. It is not different with God. These people only allow God insofar as He will serve their personal desires. They are still the ruler in their kingdom.

These people live their lives for themselves. They go to God only in times of need. God becomes a personal partner in this life whom they utilize at their whim. When things get rough, they call upon God. If they have a need, they call upon God. If things are not turning out the way they want them to, they go to God and ask Him to make it right in their own eyes. It's not God's kingdom. It's their own kingdom.

These people try to create earthly wealth, benefits, and a legacy to promote their own kingdom. They may give to God some of "their" blessings, but they see it as theirs instead of seeing themselves as stewards of what He has given to them.

These people think that God's love simply means that He loves them in their sin and affirms their sinful lifestyle and identity. To say that God loves us in our sin, in spite of our sin, and just the way we are is biblical. To say that God affirms and blesses our sinful lifestyle is not the gospel. Loving you in your sin is not saying He blesses or condones your sin. It simply is saying He does love you the way you are. The power of the gospel is that God loves you too much to allow you to live in your sinful identity. A person who lives as their own lord only wants God to be okay with and bless what they do, even when their desire goes against His holiness.

These people do not submit their lives to the obedience of Christ. They live their lives close enough to Christ to still think they are counted by Him, but they neglect to walk as one of His disciples. These people love this world and the things of this world and try to reconcile their religion with the ways of the world. These people live like the old nature, and many times it is hard to see any fruits of new birth in their life. These people are carnal and immature in the things of God. These people have no fruits of transformation but have many works of the flesh prevalent in their life.

These people also have no perspective of eternal things or any understanding of why God even placed them here for this time and place. These people do not walk out the blueprint that God has specifically made for them. They simply go about their life in the way that pleases them. They honestly think they are in charge and that they have things under control for the most part.

These people live in delusion, and many times walk away from the faith when their idea of God does not align with how their own kingdom is turning out. These people have a form of godliness but deny the application of the power of the gospel in their life. These people may or may not even be saved. If they are saved, they live as a consumer in the kingdom of God, and they only take from the Kingdom of God because they have their own to manage.

These people never experience the full identity of an intimate, abiding relationship with Christ. They never experience the joy of submission to Christ and the love and security that comes with that. They strive in their unrighteousness, never fully abiding in their true identity.

Unfortunately, in my experience, a large majority of "church" people today live in this mindset. They live according to their kingdom, according to their own rules, according to their own perspective.

Second Kingdom: Religious, Political, and Social Kingdoms

The people who lives in the second kingdom are self-righteous because they follow the rules and organizational principles upon which their kingdom was founded. They find comfort in their ability to look a certain way, believe a certain way, and align their behaviors with a certain set of beliefs. I know such people well, because I was one of them for many years—until I was introduced to an intimate, abiding relationship with Christ.

Citizens of the second kingdom do not have the joy of the Lord or of their salvation. Many in this kingdom do not subscribe to the biblical gospel. Their way to God comes through a works-based mindset. They are always striving and "doing" so they'll be accepted as part of this system. Their kingdom many times puts the traditions of men in place of, or before, the Word of God. As a result, they view manmade traditions, institutions, and entities as the objects of their religion and believe that if they adhere to the rules, they are righteous before God.

People who live in the second kingdom are distant from the heart of God. They view God much as a Deist does: they believe He is up there somewhere and that He set our world in motion, but they don't believe people are in any type of fellowship with Him. They find solace in relating to God through reason, philosophy, nature, mental assent, and intelligence.

Many in this kingdom take pride in their horizontal campaigns. They think they will change the world through social justice, politics, continuing education, and learning.

In my personal experience, the majority of people in this kingdom are not even born again. Their religion is not faith-based but intellect- and works-based. They actually reject orthodox biblical views for the progressive flavor of the day. They want to comprehend God instead of submitting to Him. Though they assent mentally to the idea of God, they rarely experience a heart connection to Him or a transformation by Him.

Christ's Kingdom: Savior Versus Lord

For you to live in Christ's kingdom and make Him Lord can only be accomplished when you are abiding in your identity in Christ.

Lordship is the portion of Christ's pattern of calling in which, I believe, the formation of a disciple begins. This is a call to die. This is the initial step that moves a believer who had called on God for salvation to now call on Him as Lord. In my opinion, you're not automatically a disciple because you believe. Many believers aren't disciples.

Lordship takes on a much heavier weight of commitment and sacrifice. There are levels of learning in the life of every believer. Discipleship will take you the rest of your life. In the process of discipleship, Christ's goal is that you, through intimacy with Him, are fully devoted to follow Him.

Salvation will cost you nothing. It is the free gift that God gives to everyone who believes (Ephesians 2:8). Discipleship will cost you everything. It is a call to die (Matthew 16:24). You no longer are living for yourself. Taking up your cross is signifying that you are a dead man walking. Your life is not your own, but Christ's (1 Corinthians 6:19–20).

> Then Jesus said to His disciples, "If anyone desires to come after Me, let him deny himself, and take up his cross, and follow Me. For whoever desires to save his life will lose it,

but whoever loses his life for My sake will find it. For what profit is it to a man if he gains the whole world, and loses his own soul? Or what will a man give in exchange for his soul?"

—Matthew 16:24–26

Imagine the look on the disciples' faces when Jesus talked about concepts like this. They knew, very well, what it meant in the physical sense to take up your cross. This was the action of a person who was sentenced to death and on their way to be executed.

Jesus' words are brutally honest. He was not using pleasantries anymore. He was inviting them to go to yet another level of revelation, commitment, and relationship. This is discipleship.

What are some characteristics of a disciple of Christ who lives in Christ's kingdom?

- Has moved past Savior and made Christ Lord of his life and has taken up his cross.

- Lives in personal abandonment and absolute trust in Christ.

- Lives in a daily posture of repentance.

- Is in an abiding relationship with Christ.

- Is a self-feeder on God's Word.

- Is a reproducer of what he has become in Christ.

- Understands the righteousness of Christ and abides in the identity that comes from that.

I believe, based on Christ's model, that a person becomes a disciple the moment they take up their cross to follow Him. Notice that He said "if" in the verse above. "If" is the determining factor as to what will happen next. Most people will not take this step.

Some will take this step the moment they experience God and will begin their discipleship journey. Others will call on Christ for salvation and, years later, will come to the place of taking up their cross to follow after Him. In my opinion, a disciple is born when he moves from viewing Jesus as Savior to Lord.

Personal Abandonment and Absolute Trust

The word *abandon* means to desert someone or to give up something.[32] When speaking about personal abandonment, you can see the heavy loss of personal identity that comes with being a disciple. When Christ calls you, He does call you to personal death and then life in Him.

> Therefore, if anyone is in Christ, he is a new creation; old things have passed away; behold, all things have become new.
> **—2 Corinthians 5:17**

> ...knowing this, that our old man was crucified with Him, that the body of sin might be done away with, that we should no longer be slaves of sin. For he who has died has been freed from sin.
> **—Romans 6:6–7**

At your spiritual new birth, you become a new creation. The old person is supposed to be buried in baptism and give way to the new person to live in Christ. This is clearly portrayed in Scripture in many different contexts. I have tried to lay this foundation in this book, as well, to help you see the power of abiding in your identity.

This goes back to the full gospel conversation. If you have been brought into the Kingdom of God in any way other than personal abandonment, then you have missed an entire portion of the power of the gospel. Abiding in your identity comes with so many benefits and blessings that we have talked about throughout this book. It also comes at the cost of personal abandonment. If you want to fully abide in your identity in Christ, it will mean forsaking utterly your old identity.

You cannot keep one foot in the identity of your old nature and one in your new nature and expect to abide in your identity in Christ. This means that you are a double-minded person, and James tells us that you cannot expect to receive anything from God if you behave that way.

Most assuredly, I say to you, unless a grain of wheat falls into the ground and dies, it remains alone; but if it dies, it produces much grain. He who loves his life will lose it, and he who hates his life in this world will keep it for eternal life. If anyone serves Me, let him follow Me; and where I am, there My servant will be also. If anyone serves Me, him My Father will honor.

—John 12:24–26

Once again, Jesus paints a clear picture of His kingdom. Unless you allow your old nature to die, you will never live in your new nature. If you try and hold on to your old nature, you will not walk in your new nature. If you let your own kingdom die in pursuit of His, you will find eternal life. It's not complicated, but it sure is difficult.

Absolute trust is the second part of this statement. I asked the Lord years ago to help me define what *absolute trust* looked like. I felt like He revealed to me that absolute trust is the very definition of faith.

> *Now faith is the substance of things hoped for, the evidence of things not seen.*
>
> *But without faith it is impossible to please Him, for he who comes to God must believe that He is, and that He is a rewarder of those who diligently seek Him.*
> **—Hebrews 11:1, 6**

Without faith, it is impossible to please God. Faith is absolute trust in God. Faith occurs when you put your confidence, belief, and hope in something that you do not physically have in your hand. If you have it in your hand, then there is no longer a need for faith. Faith is the evidence of the thing in which you are putting your hope.

Can you have pure faith with God without personal abandonment? I don't think so. If you are still focused on and confident in your abilities, then you are not sold out to the alternative: personal abandonment. To say you have faith in God but then to try to micromanage your life and hold on to all the horizontal and temporary things, proves that you don't have pure faith. I am not saying this is easy, but neither did Christ. Living the life of a disciple will go against all of your earthly, personal luxuries. This is why it is called being crucified with Christ.

Faith means letting go of all control to the King. Faith means that although things don't add up in your intellectual processing or align with your earthly pursuits, you still rest in His purpose and plans. Too many Christians have their own kingdom ideas and plans, and then they ask God to bless what they are doing and call that faith. They put all of their hopes and dreams into a plan and then tell God that this is what they want Him to do.

Absolute trust puts your visions, desires, hopes, and dreams on the altar and seeks the heart of the King in pursuit of His affections. A person abiding in their identity in Christ has a transformed heart that has new Kingdom desires and interests. Absolute trust knows that anything I have in this life is from God and for His glory. He has asked me to be a faithful steward of His resources. My life purpose is to know Christ and make Him known. There is no personal legacy. There is no personal kingdom. All of that is swallowed up in the eternal Kingdom of God. All of these earthly kingdom pursuits will be burned up eventually and what remains is what is constant. What remains is what was invested in His kingdom. What remains is what I will be judged against and rewarded for.

Absolute trust thinks eternally and not just generationally. This mindset knows that I am a part of what God has been doing in eternity and what He will continue to do in eternity. I get to be a part of that. None of it is mine. It's all His—including me.

For many are called, but few are chosen.
—Matthew 22:14

But they all, with one accord, began to make excuses.
—Luke 14:18

Many believers have every intention of becoming disciples of Christ. They make lofty plans to make that commitment at some point in the near future. Like what we read in the verses above, we see that many are called and invited to discipleship, but few choose to come. In Luke 14, we see many excuses for not answering the call.

He continues, later in this chapter, to set the bar even higher, by saying if you want to follow Him, you must be willing to hate everything else. He makes clear that the relationship between them and Him should be the most important in the world, and they should be willing to set all else aside. Every other relationship should be second to Christ.

Consider the Cost

So, likewise, whoever of you does not forsake all that he has, cannot be My disciple.
—Luke 14:33

Sadly, many preach a life of decision only and neglect to talk about a life of discipleship. People hit hard times and things don't seem to be working, and so they become disillusioned with Jesus instead of remaining devoted to

Him. Jesus will always require you to go to the next level, because He wants you to fulfill the blueprint He has for your life. This cannot happen when you are living with one foot in His family and one in the world.

Carnal Christians do not produce eternal fruit. They live like mere men, as if they had never been changed. They live in their kingdom as king and never see the fullness of their identity in Christ.

> *Now great multitudes went with Him. And He turned and said to them, "If anyone comes to Me and does not hate his father and mother, wife and children, brothers and sisters, yes, and his own life also, he cannot be My disciple. And whoever does not bear his cross and come after Me cannot be My disciple. For which of you, intending to build a tower, does not sit down first and count the cost, whether he has enough to finish it—lest, after he has laid the foundation, and is not able to finish, all who see it begin to mock him, saying, 'This man began to build and was not able to finish.' Or what king, going to make war against another king, does not sit down first and consider whether he is able with ten thousand to meet him who comes against him with twenty thousand? Or else, while the other is still a great way off, he sends a delegation and asks conditions of peace. So likewise, whoever of you does not forsake all that he has cannot be My disciple."*
> *—Luke 14:25–33*

People cannot be your identity or the reason for your existence if you want to abide in your identity in Christ. That sounds rather radical, I know. People are important and matter in this life. However, they can become an idol in place of Christ in your life. What did Jesus say about this? You can live without many horizontal things when your identity is in Christ.

Was Jesus calling His followers to hate their families and their own lives? No, Jesus was simply showing the seriousness of loving Him above all else. One of the definitions of the word *hate* in the translation can mean "to love less than." If you are going to abide in your identity and live submitted to Christ and His kingdom, you must put your love and affection first toward Him, and every other relationship must come second to Him.

Earlier in this book, we talked about how you came to Christ affects how you will live or won't live for Him. This applies here as well. Too many church leaders preach a cheap gospel and peddle a soft savior. They make the gospel out to be some easy path people can choose that culminates with a simple hand in the air and the completion of a membership class. This is not the gospel of Christ.

Too many times people do not consider the cost of discipleship as Jesus laid out. He uses the parable above to show the silliness of someone who would set out to do some huge task and not consider whether they were able to complete it. And yet we have preachers preaching every week that this Christianity thing is a simple call to a one-time quick emotional decision. There is no considering the full cost of death, personal abandonment, absolute trust, and allegiance to a new creation, a new Kingdom, and a new King.

Have you taken the time to consider the cost of discipleship? What is hindering your allegiance to your Lord and King? What kingdom are you living under?

From that time Jesus began to show to His disciples that He must go to Jerusalem, and suffer many things from the elders and chief priests and scribes, and be killed, and be raised the third day.

Then Peter took Him aside and began to rebuke Him, saying, "Far be it from You, Lord; this shall not happen to You!" But He turned and said to Peter, "Get behind Me, Satan! You are an offense to Me, for you are not mindful of the things of God, but the things of men."

—Matthew 16:21–23

What things are challenging your identity in Christ? Christ rebuked Peter and even addressed the spiritual battle and the influence Satan had on Peter in that moment. He then called out offense and a mind that was focused on the wrong things. This seems pretty severe to some, but Jesus did exactly what we should do. Anything that gets in the way of abiding in your identity should be directly dealt with. Jesus knew what He was called to do, and He was not letting anything get in the way of fulfilling His Kingly wishes.

But none of these things move me; nor do I count my life dear to myself, so that I may finish my race with joy, and the ministry which I received from the Lord Jesus, to testify to the gospel of the grace of God.
—Acts 20:24

Or do you not know that your body is the temple of the Holy Spirit who is in you, whom you have from God, and you are

not your own? For you were bought at a price; therefore,
glorify God in your body and in your spirit, which are God's.
—1 Corinthians 6:19–20

And those who are Christ's have crucified the flesh with its
passions and desires.
—Galatians 5:24

Your life is not your own. Identity is something that I think so many Christ followers still have never tapped into. It's not about what you do first, but who you are because of whose you are. You must first understand that your identity is in Christ. Your citizenship is not of this world, but in heaven.

If we are truly born again, then your life is hidden in Christ (Colossians 3:3), and you are a dead man or woman walking. You were buried with Christ in baptism, and your life is not your own. You crucify your flesh and live according to the Spirit of God. You don't govern your own life—rather, you are in Christ.

This is such a foreign concept to so many Christians whom I have talked with over my lifetime. So many are trying to identify themselves in so many things to which we can relate. They are trying to understand and be understood. This filters into every area of their lives. They are constantly trying to identify with things and people that are seemingly secure and give them some stability, if only for a moment. They have lost a huge part of being a child of God.

Allegiance to My King

I live in a constitutional republic in America that is supposed to be governed by the people. We elect public servants who represent us, and they speak on our behalf. If we don't like what they do on our behalf, we fire them and try again. This system of government has given us a list of rights and has produced a culture of people who have learned to demand those rights and put "me" first. It puts us in the driver's seat, as the captain of our own ship. It ultimately keeps pointing back to what is best for "me."

I am grateful to God to live in America, and I don't take that citizenship lightly. However, I don't think for a minute that America is my salvation or even the hope of the world. I think many Christians are American first and Christian second. We think that God and the world revolves around us. This simply is not the case. We limit God to our Western cultural worldview and have a hard time seeing outside of this. I think a lot of us in America have become arrogant, self-centered, and spoiled, and we have lost sight of the powerful gift that we have been given in this season of religious freedom and freedom of speech.

I have listened to the arguments that if we lose our religious freedom, then we will slip into a "dark ages" season. I have heard people declare that a certain political candidate is our only hope. They point to different things like religious freedom. My question is, if we lost our religious freedom or our freedom of speech, would that stop God's purposes? I can hear it now, God speaking to Jesus, "Oh my, Jesus, if we lose America, we will be unable to accomplish our plans that we set in motion long before America was here." What? Have we looked at the biblical history of the nation of Israel? When that nation turned against God, He moved and allowed the earthly, physical, governmental, and political parts of that great nation to be removed. He didn't put up with it, and He is the same God now that He was then. America, we had better take note.

Nationalism Is Not Kingdom-Minded

Some people have made America out to be the medium by which God will execute His purposes on the earth. I love that God has used America and can continue to use this nation, as He has with so many others over the centuries. However, America is not the hope of the world, and putting your faith and hope in a nationalistic human savior is not Kingdom-minded.

Many people think of America as the "United States of Jesus." But the warnings are clear: "Think of American civil religion in biblical terms: America is Israel. The Revolution is our Exodus. The Declaration of Independence, Bill of Rights, and Constitution compose our canon of sacred scripture. Abraham Lincoln is our Moses. Independence Day is our Easter. Our national enemies are our Satan. Benedict Arnold is our Judas. The Founding Fathers are our apostles. Taxes are our tithes. Patriotic songs are our hymnal. The Pledge of Allegiance is our sinner's prayer. And the president is our preacher, which is why throughout the history of the office our leaders have referred to 'God' without any definition or clarification, allowing people to privately import their own understanding of a higher power."[33]

This may sound ludicrous, yet I have seen this attitude over and over in the American church, especially in the Bible Belt, where I live. People think that to be a Christian is American and that America is automatically a Christian nation. I don't want to get into the many different debated sides of this conversation, but America was not birthed to be a Christian nation. America was set up to be a religiously free nation. This meant that you would be free to practice any religion that you wanted. Many of the Founding Fathers were monotheists but they were far from being biblical Christians.

When you try to make America out to be the savior, you lose sight of the sovereignty of God. Again, God can use America to advance His kingdom, but His kingdom is so much bigger than one nation. Let us remove God from our boxes and self-promoting nationalistic ideas and let God be God. His kingdom is forever and it will outlast any one individual nation.

> *See that you do not refuse Him who speaks. For if they did not escape who refused Him who spoke on earth, much more shall we not escape if we turn away from Him who speaks from heaven, whose voice then shook the earth; but now He has promised, saying, "Yet once more I shake not only the earth, but also heaven." Now this, "Yet once more," indicates the removal of those things that are being shaken, as of things that are made, that the things which cannot be shaken may remain.*
> **—Hebrews 12:25–27**

I don't wish that America will ever be removed or even changed in a lot of ways that many are proposing, but I would not lose my hope if it does. I think there would be a huge vacuum effect on the global scene if America was not here or if it changed from the values on which it was founded. However, God is bigger than America. God got His bidding done in the earth long before America was here. Most of Church history has been lived out under religious persecution and without religious freedom. Imagine that: God worked even when it seemed like the conditions were not best for Him to operate! I want to state that again: Most of Church history has been lived out under persecution. Even in the early Church, we saw that the gospel thrived when it was most fought against.

Currently, much of the global Church is under great persecution, and yet in those areas the gospel is spreading like wildfire. The fastest-growing churches on the globe today are in Iran, where people are killed for converting to Christianity. [34]

And how does this look for us Christians in America? Do we have more faith in America or God? Sure, God can use America, as He can any nation or group of people, but He is not limited. He is God. What is God's perspective?

Woe to those who call evil good, and good evil; who put darkness for light, and light for darkness; who put bitter for sweet, and sweet for bitter!

—Isaiah 5:20

> *For David, after he had served his own generation by the will of God, fell asleep, was buried with his fathers, and saw corruption...*
>
> *—Acts 13:36*

I think many Christians view the Kingdom of God as a constitutional republic. We think we have say-so, but that is not how God works. The Kingdom of God is not governed by the people, but is a theocracy. God is the King, and He rules and reigns supreme. We are called to serve Him and obey His words. We don't get to pick and choose the words we like and simply discard the others.

Are we willing to serve the will of God for our generation? Look at the people of Jeremiah's day. They were promised a future and a hope in the midst of exile and judgment—which God had not only allowed but also initiated because they had turned away from Him (Jeremiah 29:11).

I think it is very presumptuous to think we know all the plans that God has. We cannot picture a world without certain things we have grown accustomed to, and we cling to them as if God's purposes hung on those things remaining. I don't know all of God's plans and purposes, but I do know *Him*.

> *And who is he who will harm you if you become followers of what is good? But even if you should suffer for righteousness' sake, you are blessed. "And do not be afraid of their threats, nor be troubled." But sanctify the Lord God in your hearts, and always be ready to give a defense to everyone who asks you a reason for the hope that is in you, with meekness and fear; having a good conscience, that when they defame you as evildoers, those who revile your good*

conduct in Christ may be ashamed. For it is better, if it is the will of God, to suffer for doing good than for doing evil.
—1 Peter 3:13-17

Where Does This Leave Us?

If we understand and live in our identity and see things through God's perspective, we can seek, pursue, and see the Father's heart to view our world through that lens. Wake up every day and ask the Lord to show you His heart in your decisions. Prayerfully navigate His Word. Be a steward to sanctify the Word of God in your heart and have a defense for the hope in you. Live in personal abandonment and absolute trust in God, knowing that He is the Author and Finisher of your faith (Hebrews 12:2). When hell is breaking loose around you, dig into your identity, getting His perspective and hearing His heart. Love the hell out of people. Love covers a multitude of sins (1 Peter 4:8). Love allows us to look past our disagreements and agree on the Father's heart.

If you have the Father's heart, you can pray and vote your conscience. You can speak up where needed and be silent where needed. Don't let people, agendas, political parties, evangelical leaders, patriots, or any other voices influence your heart after God. Be cautious what voices you are allowing to speak into your life. Every voice has a purpose and an agenda. Make sure your anchor and center is Christ, His Word, His identity, His perspective, and His heart. Do not be pulled away into intellectual deception that goes against the peace in your heart from God.

Take every thought and influence in your world captive to the Word of God (2 Corinthians 10:5).

> *Therefore we do not lose heart. Even though our outward man is perishing, yet the inward man is being renewed day by day. For our light affliction, which is but for a moment, is working for us a far more exceeding and eternal weight of glory, while we do not look at the things which are seen, but at the things which are not seen. For the things which are seen are temporary, but the things which are not seen are eternal.*
> **—2 Corinthians 4:16–18**

> *For you did not receive the spirit of bondage again to fear, but you received the Spirit of adoption by whom we cry out, "Abba, Father." The Spirit Himself bears witness with our spirit that we are children of God, and if children, then heirs—heirs of God and joint heirs with Christ, if indeed we suffer with Him, that we may also be glorified together.*
> **—Romans 8:15–17**

> *And because you are sons, God has sent forth the Spirit of His Son into your hearts, crying out, "Abba, Father!" Therefore you are no longer a slave but a son, and if a son, then an heir of God through Christ.*
> **—Galatians 4:6–7**

Remember, the Church is not a chapel, meeting place, set of rules, group of laws, denomination, or any other temporary thing. The Church is made up of the ones who abide in Christ, walk in His identity, gain His perspective, and live out the Father's heart. The Church is you and me being ambassadors for Christ, having Christ imploring the world through us to come to Him, reconciling God to people. The Church is the fragrance of God (2 Corinthians 2:15). The Church is the books and epistles found in the Scriptures. The Church is the medium by which God chose to preserve a posterity of His glory in this earth.

Stand up, Church! Stop acting like something you are not and start acting like you are the sons and daughters of God. Stop engaging in earthly sensual warfare and take up the full armor of God and engage in spiritual warfare (Ephesians 6:10–18). Stop focusing on the temporal, fading things and look to the eternal, unseen things. We are a part of an unshakable kingdom with an eternal citizenship.

What are some of your excuses as to why you have not made Christ Lord and submitted to His kingdom? "This is just how I am" is a common excuse. If you truly believe this statement, then you must wrestle with the question of whether God created you that way or if you are living in your sinful nature.

If you believe that God created you a certain way, a way that goes against His Word, then you are deceived and living in the wrong identity. God's Word reveals His identity to humanity. He does not do things contrary to His Word. This would make Him a liar and not God. If, however, you believe you were born a certain way and are struggling to align that with God's Word, then you are on the correct journey. Welcome to the human race.

We are all born with sinful tendencies. Being born into a sinful world with a sinful nature is not a prescription for how God wants you to live. Our sin nature is a simple fruit of the fall of humanity. Christ did not come to affirm our sinful natures but redeem us from them. He came to restore our fellowship with the Father.

Being born with sinful tendencies proves your need for God's grace that much more. Being born with sinful pursuits is more evidence of needing this revelation to abide in your identity in Christ and not your sinful nature. Do not fall for the lie that you are the way you are and continue to live in your sinful nature. Dare to accept the call to discipleship, the call to die. Dare to abide in your identity in Christ with personal abandonment and absolute trust. This will change everything.

WORKBOOK

Chapter Eight Questions

Question: Describe the different kingdoms that Christians and professing Christians might serve. What is the difference between accepting Christ as Savior and following Him as Lord? Which kingdom are you pursuing?

_____

_____

_____

_____

_____

_____

_____

_____

_____

_____

_____

Question: What are characteristics of a disciple? Why do some who have been converted fail to become disciples? What is the cost of discipleship?

_____

_____

_____

_____

_____

_____

_____

_____

_____

_____

_____

Question: What should be the attitude of a disciple toward his/her earthly nation, particularly in America?

_____

_____

_____

_____

_____

_____

_____

_____

_____

_____

_____

_____

_____

Action: Study the life of one of the "heroes of the faith" whose life modeled paying the cost of discipleship (e.g., Adoniram Judson, Hudson Taylor, Amy Carmichael, Dietrich Bonhoeffer, C.S. Lewis). What was the cost of discipleship for this person? How was it both a decision and a process in their life? What can you learn from their example?

_____

_____

_____

_____

_____

_____

_____

_____

_____

_____

_____

_____

Journal: Meditate on Matthew 16:24–26 and journal using the STAR method. Have you counted the cost, taken
up your cross, and made the decision to be Christ's disciple?

Chapter Eight Notes

CHAPTER NINE

Living in Holiness

Unless sin is seen to be sin, grace will never be seen to be grace.[35]

—C.H. Spurgeon

Men do not reject the Bible because it contradicts itself, but because it contradicts them.[36]

—E. Paul Hovey

It's past time the Church started talking about holiness. In the Church, we talk a lot about overcoming sin, dealing with personal issues, and handing problem areas over to God, but we rarely take it one step further. We rarely talk about holiness—despite this being a key point in Paul's writings.

I believe that many Christians would be shocked to understand the biblical call to holiness. I believe that many would reject holiness because of our love of sinful things. When I see people passionate about the things of God but then equally passionate about sinful behavior and the things of this world, it causes me to pause and question the fruit. Can there be true gospel transformation without Kingdom fruit?

Many Bible scholars will argue that our holiness is not for this earthly life but for eternity in heaven. In turn, many Christians take this as a "pass," or a reason not to pursue holiness on earth.

In this chapter, I want to show the overwhelming scriptural commands and prescriptions for you to walk in holiness before God, now, on this earth. Part of abiding in your identity in Christ is this wonderful fruit of transformation called holiness. Many of the scriptures we have used throughout this book have affirmed that God has called you to be holy.

If God asks something of you, He also gives you the power to accomplish that thing, in Him. This is the theme of this book. You are not meant to do any of this life alone, separate from Him. Walking in holiness takes the same faith that you appropriated for salvation and sanctification. Enough with the excuses about all the things we weak, frail humans cannot do. Let us examine who we are in Him and what He empowers us to do.

My experience with thousands of people over the past many years in ministry, as well as my personal story, prove to me the power of transformation in Christ that produces the fruit of holiness. When we focus on sanctification, or holiness, separate from an intimate, abiding relationship with Christ, we once again drive people to self-righteousness. People who are not abiding in their identity in Christ but who see the biblical commands of obedience and holiness will eventually wear themselves out by trying hard in their own ability to please God. This is the opposite of how God desires this to be. Holiness and obedience are direct fruits of abiding in righteousness.

I use the example of what I call treadmill Christianity. When you run on a treadmill, you work up a good sweat and become physically tired, and yet you never really go anywhere. No matter how many times that belt on which you are running cycles around, you still are in the same place you started.

When you try to obey God or live in holiness outside of this righteousness we have been exploring, you will have many works that look good, but you never get any further down the road of spiritual maturity. You get good at managing your sin and behavior, but that eventually gives way and you fall down and bloody yourself all up. If you have a strong will, you will get up over and over and try harder, thinking each time that things will be different. But you eventually end up in the same place, falling and all bloodied up in self-righteousness, sin, and bad choices.

When you abide in your identity in Christ, He transforms your heart from the inside, and then the fruits of that are seen outwardly. He changes your desires and gives you new ones. Your love of sin is transformed into love for God. The idols you once worshiped fall by the wayside as God becomes your singularly focused object of worship.

For it pleased the Father that in Him all the fullness should dwell, and by Him to reconcile all things to Himself, by Him, whether things on earth or things in heaven, having made

> *peace through the blood of His cross. And you, who once were alienated and enemies in your mind by wicked works, yet now He has reconciled in the body of His flesh through death,* **to present you holy, and blameless, and above reproach in His sight—if indeed you continue in the faith, grounded and steadfast, and are not moved away from the hope of the gospel which you heard, which was preached to every creature under heaven,** *of which I, Paul, became a minister.*
> **—Colossians 1:19–23, emphasis mine**

Here are some questions on holiness that I want to explore in this chapter:

- Do you know what biblical holiness is?

- Does God ask you to live holy?

- Is it even possible to live holy this side of heaven?

Typical Assumptions

Some assumptions we typically make as church leaders are that the people in our sphere of influence have the same value system and moral standards that we have. We assume that everyone in our church is on the same page as to what defines sin, grace, obedience, and holiness. However, in my experience as a church leader, I have come to understand that we are *not* all on the same page within the church context. Here are some of the assumptions we tend to believe about the people in our congregations:

Among us there is an automatic and understood consensus about what sin is (what is right and what is wrong). We cannot afford to assume that this is true.

Among us there is an automatic and understood consensus about what grace looks like in our practical, day-to-day lives.

Among us there is an automatic and understood consensus about what holiness is and whether or not we would even embrace holiness if we fully knew what it was.

> The nature of Christ's salvation is woefully misrepresented by the present-day evangelist. He announces a savior from hell rather than a savior from sin. And that is why so many are fatally deceived, for there are multitudes that wish to escape the Lake of Fire who have no desire to be delivered from their carnality and worldliness.[37]
>
> **—A.W. Pink**

> *Awake to righteousness, and do not sin; for some do not have the knowledge of God. I speak this to your shame.*
> **—1 Corinthians 15:34**

What Is Biblical Holiness?

Righteousness is directly related to holiness. Until you wake up in your understanding and your walk in righteousness, sin will dominate you. Living in holiness is not something you can strive and accomplish, but rather it is a fruit of an intimate, abiding relationship with Christ.

Paul told the Corinthian believers that it was shameful that some did not know holiness was a fruit of a believer.

How much more would Paul stress this point of disappointment and rebuke if he showed up on the modern-day Christian scene here in America? I think he would be devastated at the lack of understanding of holiness in today's church.

Many in the church are waiting for a sovereign move of God to bring revival to us, when I think God is waiting for us to appropriate what He has already done at the cross. He desires that we walk by faith in the righteousness that Christ provided in His victory over sin. Abiding in your identity empowers you to live free from sin.

Although righteousness cannot be earned, it should produce a change in us that leads us into good works and eventual holiness before God. This is a process that happens over the period of your lifetime. Carefully read the next verse from Romans 6. Let that knowledge move you through the rest of this chapter.

For sin shall not have dominion over you, for you are not under law but under grace. What then? Shall we sin because we are not under law but under grace? Certainly not! Do you not know that to whom you present yourselves slaves to obey, you are that one's slaves whom you obey, whether of sin leading to death, or of obedience leading to righteousness? But God be thanked that though you were slaves of sin, yet you obeyed from the heart that form of doctrine to which you were delivered. And having been set free from sin, you became slaves of righteousness. I speak in human terms because of the weakness of your flesh. For just as you presented your members as slaves of uncleanness, and of lawlessness leading to more lawlessness, so now present your members as slaves of righteousness for holiness. For when you were slaves of sin, you were free in regard to righteousness. What fruit did you have then in the things of which you are now ashamed? For the end of those things is death. But now having been set free from sin, and having become slaves of God, you have your fruit to holiness, and the end, everlasting life. For the wages of sin is death, but the gift of God is eternal life in Christ Jesus our Lord.

—Romans 6:14–23

Does God Ask You to Live Holy?

The standard of God is to live a sinless life. His standard is holiness. You will fall short and sin, but that should not be the standard by which you live (Romans 3:23). There is a huge difference between living a lifestyle of sin and falling short.

I have a friend who heard a professed Christian talking about how he related more to the works of the flesh than to the fruits of the Spirit. The person who told me this was amazed by the conversation and wondered how a Bible-believing Christian could live like that.

This is a huge part of the problem. The person in question had been taught that he was just a lowly sinner and that he could not control his sin nature this side of heaven—therefore, he lived that way. Very few have been taught about the dominion we can have over sin when we abide in righteousness.

The theme of you playing a part in your sanctification and transformation is echoed once again in Romans 6 above. Before Christ, you chose by your will to indulge in your sinful and fleshly tendencies. You were a slave to sin. Sin had dominion over you. Every choice you made was carnal.

But now, under grace, you have the ability to sustain obedience to the will of God. This new life and transformed heart allow you to choose to live in righteousness for holiness. I cannot tell you how excited this makes me and how this chapter is such a powerful piece of abiding in identity!

For too long, we have taught believers that the battle against sin is not something that can be overcome on this side of heaven. This should not be. Our identity in Christ gives us new affections and fruits of the Holy Spirit. He lives in you and will empower you to live in obedience and holiness.

Praise God for this blessing! This is a huge part of the gospel message. The wages of sin amount only to death, but the free gift of God is obedience, holiness, and everlasting life (Romans 6:23).

Is It Possible to Live a Holy Life?
What If We Miss the Mark?

The three passages of Scripture below paint a similar picture as that of Romans 6. You will miss the mark, even as a born-again believer. That is not being denied. These verses are not talking about a non-believer accepting salvation, but rather they are speaking to a believer who has sinned and recognized where he fell short. When he repents, there is a forgiveness and cleansing by God. Amen to this!

If we say that we have no sin, we deceive ourselves, and the truth is not in us. If we confess our sins, He is faithful and just to forgive us our sins and to cleanse us from all un-righteousness. If we say that we have not sinned, we make Him a liar, and His word is not in us.

—*1 John 1:8–10*

My little children, these things I write to you, so that you may not sin. And if anyone sins, we have an Advocate with the Father, Jesus Christ the righteous. And He Himself is the propitiation for our sins, and not for ours only but also for the whole world. Now by this we know that we know Him, if we keep His commandments. He who says, "I know Him," and does not keep His commandments, is a liar, and the truth is not in him. But whoever keeps His word, truly the love of God is perfected in him. By this we know that we are in Him. He who says he abides in Him ought himself also to walk just as He walked.

—*1 John 2:1–6*

Whoever abides in Him does not sin. Whoever sins has nei-ther seen Him nor known Him. Little children, let no one deceive you. He who practices righteousness is righteous, just as He is righteous. He who sins is of the devil, for the devil has sinned from the beginning. For this purpose the Son of God was manifested, that He might destroy the works of the devil. Whoever has been born of God does not sin, for His seed remains in him; and he cannot sin, because he has been born of God.

—*1 John 3:6–9*

You will sin and fall short at times, and the Bible is clear on that. However, the standard of God is not to re-main in a lifestyle of sin. Whoever abides in Him does not live in sin. When you sin, as an abider in Christ, you will quickly repent and accept the gift of forgiveness. Sinful lifestyles should not be the norm for someone who abides in Christ. The works of the devil have been destroyed in you, and you are not bound to live as a slave to sin any longer. This is amazingly good news!

I love the picture of our loving advocate, Jesus Christ, before the Father. We don't have to cower in shame and sulk around in sackcloth and ashes. Someone who abides in righteousness will quickly run to God instead of away from Him. If, when you sin, you run from God in shame, I would challenge that you struggle with your identity. When you know the Father's heart, sin will convict you and cause regret and godly sorrow. This will drive you to God in repentance, not away from Him.

Are you accepting this amazing news from God to you? Do you see the power you have over a sinful lifestyle when you abide in your identity in Christ? God calls you to holiness, and therefore He will make a provision for you to walk in it. If God commands it, then He will provide a way for you to live in it.

> But you are a chosen generation, a royal priesthood, a holy nation, His own special people, that you may proclaim the praises of Him who called you out of darkness into His marvelous light; who once were not a people but are now the people of God, who had not obtained mercy but now have obtained mercy.
> **—1 Peter 2:9–10**

You are called to be a part of this holy, called-out, people of God. You are identified by His presence and holiness. You have been called out of darkness. You once were without identity and lost in this world, but now you have your identity in Him.

> *But the fruit of the Spirit is love, joy, peace, longsuffering, kindness, goodness, faithfulness, gentleness, self-control. Against such there is no law. And those who are Christ's have crucified the flesh with its passions and desires. If we live in the Spirit, let us also walk in the Spirit.*
> **—Galatians 5:22–25**

When you abide in Christ, you have the Holy Spirit living in you. He empowers you unto holiness. His fruits should be clearly evident in your life. If you do not relate to the attributes in the verse above, then I would encourage you to examine what identity you are living in. If you are Christ's, then you will live in a posture of crucifying your flesh and the passions and desires for sin that once ruled you. You should experience the fruits of the Holy Spirit as a direct result of your transformed heart.

The mantra of today's world rings eerily similar to Aleister Crowley's Thelemic mysticism's mantra: "Do what thou wilt."[38] This is opposite of what God asks, commands, and empowers us to do. Where in Scripture does God give you permission to live in a lifestyle of sin? There is no excuse for us as transformed sons and daughters of God to live a lifestyle of sin. He clearly has given us the directives, authority, and power to live a life in the Spirit through the crucified flesh.

I am continually amazed at how deceived we can be as human beings, myself included. People typically don't want to see the truth—instead, they want to see their version of the truth. People search the Scriptures to affirm their embedded theology and their already held beliefs. They want the Word to tolerate and affirm their identity rather than define it.

The Word is supposed to wash us, cleanse us, and renew our minds to God's thoughts, not simply affirm our own belief systems. We combat error, deception, and temptation with the truth of God's Word. The Bible tells us over and over to "not be deceived" (Luke 21:8; 1 Corinthians 6:9; 1 Corinthians 15:33; Galatians 6:7; James 1:16).

If you claim to be abiding in your identity in Christ but you are unloving, living a lifestyle of sin, are racist, homophobic, stingy, and consumed with worldly things, then I would say you are not abiding in your identity in Christ. You are still living after the fleshly old nature. You have not allowed your transformed heart to dominate the rest of your person. You have not renewed your mind to God's way. I am not talking about the occasional fleshly moment, but a lifestyle—works of the flesh versus fruits of the Spirit.

But he who does the truth comes to the light, that his deeds may be clearly seen, that they have been done in God."
—John 3:21

The points below show the cycle or progression of our walk with Christ.

Repentance and brokenness. Our realization of our sinful nature should drive us to seek a solution. Unfortunately, many people find the wrong solution in the wrong places. Many churches have offered the wrong solution as well, a religious legalism that is not freedom but further bondage. This leaves people disillusioned with the church, and they see no hope in the real church that Christ is building.

We must be cautious that we do not become like some members of the early Church who desired Gentile Christians to be brought under Jewish Law, which was equated to religious bondage instead of freedom in Christ. Legalistic churches bring Gentiles from one bondage into another, and that is not our intention. Recognition of our sin will hopefully drive us to better understand God's grace.

> *Blessed are the poor in spirit, for theirs is the kingdom of heaven.*
> **—Matthew 5:3**

Grace. Grace is God's unmerited favor along with His empowerment. When we experience God's grace, it is not merely to save us with His favor, but to empower us to live in such a way that honors Him. Many have taken grace and made it a license to sin. Some have gone from legalism and bypassed Christian liberty, moving right to a license to sin. Grace should cause us to live in a lifestyle of repentance. God's grace should drive us to obedience, not away from it.

> *For the grace of God that brings salvation has appeared to all men, teaching us that, denying ungodliness and worldly lusts, we should live soberly, righteously, and godly in the present age, looking for the blessed hope and glorious appearing of our great God and Savior Jesus Christ, who gave Himself for us, that He might redeem us from every lawless deed and purify for Himself His own special people, zealous for good works. Speak these things, exhort, and rebuke with all authority. Let no one despise you.*
>
> *—Titus 2:11–15*

Obedience. Living a Holy Spirit-empowered life that produces obedience to God and His Word is a direct fruit of experiencing His grace. Many grace movements today view any type of call to obedience as legalism and therefore run from it. They run from the very thing grace is driving them toward. When we live in God's grace, it creates the liberty to choose obedience. True liberty in Christ lived out creates obedience, not excess. The only way to walk out pure obedience is through God's grace. Grace moves you to good works, not to sin. A self-righteous person can obey out of his or her will, but this is not a fruit of grace. A person who has received and lives in the grace of God will walk in obedience to His Word.

> *For by grace you have been saved through faith, and that not of yourselves; it is the gift of God, not of works, lest anyone should boast. For we are His workmanship, created in Christ Jesus for good works, which God prepared beforehand that we should walk in them.*
>
> *—Ephesians 2:8–10*

Words from God to us that say "do this" or "don't do this" are not given to us from our loving Father to spoil our fun and restrict our joy, but out of His desire that our joy would be fulfilled. Sometimes the process is painful at first, but God wants us to be brought to genuine fulfillment—so that we would be kept from harm and needless pain would be prevented. Something that I know about the character of God and our relationship to Him is that if God said it, there is a benefit to me in my obedience. Obedience keeps me from consequences, both seen and unseen.

Holiness. Walking out obedience produces holiness, which is what God desires for all of us. This holiness is a product of the previous three. God clearly tells us in Scripture that we are to live in holiness. This is not a suggestion, but a command. In and of ourselves, we cannot walk in holiness. It takes God's empowerment through His grace and by the Holy Spirit, as well as our responding to that empowerment in obedience. Holiness is wholeness in God.

> *Flee sexual immorality. Every sin that a man does is outside the body, but he who commits sexual immorality sins against his own body. Or do you not know that your body is the temple of the Holy Spirit who is in you, whom you have from God, and you are not your own? For you were bought at a price; therefore, glorify God in your body and in your spirit, which are God's.*
> **—1 Corinthians 6:18–20**

A Matter of Trust

The current belief trend in our culture is that morality is relative to a person's situation, belief, and lusts. There are no moral absolutes. No one can say what is right or what is wrong for another person.

However, the gospel tells us the opposite. It says to not go by slippery places because you will fall, and you will be hurt. It says that God will send His grace to you, but there will be painful consequences.

Years ago, we lived at the end of the cul-de-sac in a quiet neighborhood. There was a little island in the middle of the road where the kids loved to play. Even though there was very little traffic on our street, we did not allow our young kids to play in the street unless we were out there watching them. We never restricted their ability to play in the street to spoil their fun or because we were mean-spirited. It was quite the contrary. We had witnessed many times when vehicles would use our street to do a fast turnaround. Many of these vehicles did not pay much attention to the kids and were going entirely too fast to stop if they had to.

Much like God does with us, we did not restrict their playing in the road to hurt them. We did it as loving parents who knew what was best for them at the time. They had no idea the amount of danger they could be in if they played there without supervision. Something that I know about the character of God and our relationship is that if God said it, there is a benefit to me in my obedience, and I must trust Him in that. He knows what is best for me. He is all-knowing and has a perfect plan for my life. He sees things that there is no way I can see from my perspective. I must learn to understand His nature and heart for me, and then in personal abandonment and absolute trust, I must allow Him to lead me. If I trust Him, then I know that what He asks of me is good, even if it can be sometimes painful or unexplained. Do you have this confidence in your relationship with God?

Another parenting example of this involves my daughter. We were driving down the interstate one day, and it began to pour down rain out of nowhere. We ended up hydroplaning off the interstate, down a hill, and into the woods. We were all taken by ambulance to the nearest hospital.

While there, my daughter seemed to have the most concerning issues, and so I went with her into one room and my wife another. During all of the tests and prodding and X-rays, a lot of fear crept in. They needed to run some tests on her, and she would not let them. At one point, they had four nurses trying to hold her down for a procedure, but she was not having it. Eventually, they asked me to help or they would have to use medicine to help calm her enough to do the procedure.

I held her tight and whispered into her ear that Daddy was there and that it was going to be okay. She was screaming so loud in pain, *"Daddy! It hurts! Make them stop!"* I was crying and telling her it was going to be okay. It was a very traumatic experience for all of us. I assured her that though it was painful, these things were needed to help her in her healing process.

It all worked out ultimately, and I learned a valuable lesson that day. Sometime later, the Lord showed me that how she responded to the pain was how I respond many times to the things I face in my life. I am fearful, scared, and don't understand all that God is doing, so I cry out in desperation to ask Him to intervene. He showed me that He has me wrapped in His arms like I did my daughter. Although I don't fully understand the process and the pain that sometimes comes with the process, if I am abiding in my identity in Christ, it will all work out for my good and God's glory.

Are you still perpetuating the behaviors of your former life instead of identifying with your new identity in Christ? We were not made to live in the flesh or the soul but out of the Spirit of God within our transformed hearts.

Seasons or Patterns?

As you examine your life in light of the topic of this book, what do you see? Ask yourself if the things in your life are seasons or patterns. All of us go through seasons. They can be good, bad, and horrible. The Bible speaks about the purpose of seasons. God allows seasons in your life to refine, prune, discipline, and bless you. When you abide in your identity in Christ, the seasons will matter because you will have the perspective of your Heavenly Father.

On the other side of seasons are patterns. If you seem to live in the same patterns over and over, then it is worth examining your life in light of your redemption. Like the children of Israel in the Old Testament, we see what many scholars call cycles of apostasy. These were patterns that seemed to plague this group over many generations. They would turn away from God. God would bring judgment to them. They would turn back to Him. He would restore them. Then they would go back to turning away from Him again to idols. These patterns were more than a simple season.

What things in your life are causing sinful cycles that detract from who you are in Christ? What patterns could you acknowledge as harmful to your identity in Christ? What might be the root cause of these patterns that needs to be addressed so you can live in freedom in Christ?

Have you found yourself in any of these harmful patterns: allowing sin to turn you away from God, bad relationships, offense and bitterness, being hurt by others, spiritual apathy?

If you are not able to identify certain patterns of behavior, then you will never be able to address what is causing them and you will never find healing and deliverance.

God's love and righteousness are without condition. God's blessings are conditional.

Many times, we give Satan too much credit. Sure, he comes to steal, kill, and destroy (John 10:10). Sure, he has some power and can cause a lot of sorrow in this world.

Remember in chapter 6 ("Renew Your Mind"), when we looked at James 1? It was not Satan that was causing the issues, but our own enticement unto sin. I'm reminded of Matthew 13:1–23 and Jeremiah 4:3–4, which tell us clearly that we are to be careful how and where we sow. This includes breaking up the fallow ground and avoiding sowing into thorns. This fallow ground and thorny soil can be patterns that keep us from progressing in our growth in Christ.

Then Elijah said to all the people, "Come near to me." So all the people came near to him. And he repaired the altar of the LORD that was broken down. And Elijah took twelve stones, according to the number of the tribes of the sons of Jacob, to whom the word of the LORD had come, saying, "Israel shall be your name." Then with the stones he built an altar in the name of the LORD; and he made a trench around the altar large enough to hold two seahs of seed.
—1 Kings 18:30–32

The word used here for "repaired" is *rapha* (rawfaw), which means "to heal, abate, cease, consume, draw toward evening (fade away), forsake, leave, let alone."[39]

I love this passage, because it shows that Elijah both repaired and built his relationship with God.

Sometimes moving on from where you are to where God is taking you will require a change in your life. At times, that change will be healing or repair. At times, it will be removing yourself from the situation or from past hurts. And other times, it will require a brand-new altar or foundation. Only God knows exactly what you need in your personal life, and as you abide in Him, He desires to reveal this to you.

Amazing Grace

I agree that many religious people lack the power of pure gospel transformation, and so they rely upon such things as behavior modification to move their agendas along. However, when you preach the gospel that Christ instituted, it comes with a standard of holiness—not for us to make ourselves right, but because we are right in Him. If you preach works, holiness, or behavior modification to get into God's good graces, then that is a false gospel.

However, once we experience the grace of God, it compels and empowers us to live holy, as God does. Not to be right but because we are right. We now have the ability to overcome sin and an orphan mentality. We have the access to live in pure love with our Father. We have been translated from slaves of sin to slaves of righteousness. There is such a fine line in this topic, and many have scribbled all over that line and come up with other ways to define God's grace.

I think many in the modern grace movement have simply rebelled, not only against all the wrong in the church, but against God Himself. They are self-justified in their actions, because they feel so wronged by the religious bondage they were in for so many years. They hate the prodigal son who stayed home and lived in the father's house but was in bondage, and yet they are living a lifestyle free from the Father's house. They are the first prodigal who has not returned home. They have allowed their passion against religion to hinder their relationship with their Father.

Two wrongs don't make a right. In my experience, humans tend to live in extremes. We move from one end of the pendulum swing to the complete opposite side, missing the very balanced truth for which we are actually longing. The very thing that they disdained about religion, they have become, only on the opposite end of the spectrum. This is dangerous and cavalier.

When you move the moral line outside of the confines of a sovereign and holy God, you are left with a standard that never stops moving, based on the fruits of depravity in humanity.

Just like if you preach works or behavior modification to look as if you're right in Christ, I think when you remove holiness as the godly standard that grace empowers us unto, it is just as religious—but on the opposite extreme. Paul rebuked the Galatian church for beginning their spiritual transformation on the correct path but derailing when they tried to be perfect by going back and living according to the Law to stay righteous (Galatians 1:6–10).

It was to this very church that he talked about the fruits of the Spirit and the works of the flesh (Galatians 5:16–26). He did not water down either list. He pointed to holiness as the outflow of the Spirit's work in our lives.

Why is this so hard for us to see in light of our freedom? God has graced us with freedom from sin, not freedom from the standard of holiness. Not freedom from good works. Not freedom from truth. He freed us unto holiness, unto good works, and unto truth. Again, not to be righteous, but because we are righteous.

Just like the Galatian church, many modern grace teachers have traded one form of religious bondage for another. They desire a lifestyle free from accountability and any form of standard. In my personal experience, I have seen and known hundreds of people who now live in bondage to a sinful lifestyle because they live in the other extreme. They think they are free, but they live in bondage, and it doesn't have to be that way.

Bearing Fruit

In my study of the New Testament teaching on grace, I never see where the Bible uses grace to lower a standard of fruits. I see just the opposite. We are called to have fruits of holiness because we are connected to the Vine of Christ. Our Father disciplines us as a loving dad to develop our maturity. He is the Vinedresser, who prunes us so we will produce fruit that remains (John 15:1–8).

We have a righteousness that is from God and His grace that we did not earn or work for. This righteousness allows us to be seated in heavenly places with God at His right hand and place of authority (Ephesians 2:1–10). I see grace as upping the standard. This is not behavior modification or legalism. It is the way that God set it all up to work.

We were created for good works in Christ, and grace is that access and empowerment. These good works are not like those of a servant or a slave, but like those of a son who honors his Father and knows that when he walks in obedience, he can accomplish great things for the Kingdom. This person has come to the revelation that God loves them the way they are and has good planned for them. They want to honor the Father by obeying His truth and walking in holiness to become who God defines them to be.

The moment we affirm people in their sin or their identity outside of Christ, we quickly move toward heresy and false doctrines. Compromising truth involves preaching another gospel contrary to the one given by Christ. If you tolerate sin in your own life or in the lives of others in the name of "love," then you are not abiding in your identity in Christ. Theological issues can be debated and lived out differently, but truth is truth, and compromising it only dilutes it.

Don't lower your standard of holiness for any reason. Some lower the standard because they have not fully grasped what God has done for them. Others lower the standard to live a lifestyle of sin that is, in their minds, justified by God because He is like that. They cheapen the grace of God. Search the Scriptures today and see what the Holy Spirit reveals to you about the grace of God. Take off your goggles of religion and remove your embedded theology long enough to take an honest, unbiased look at God's grace and live in that. His grace is enough.

Chapter Nine Questions

Question: What is biblical holiness, and why is it vital for every believer? How does it differ from legalism and being judgmental?

_____

_____

_____

_____

_____

_____

_____

_____

_____

_____

_____

Question: How will the believer who is walking in their proper identity in Christ respond when they discover sin in their life? How does a relationship of trust in your Heavenly Father inform and encourage your obedience and holiness?

_____

_____

_____

_____

_____

_____

_____

_____

_____

_____

_____

Question: Are you walking in biblical balance, or are you like the ever-swinging pendulum? Has reaction to one extreme in Christian culture driven you to the opposite, equally dangerous extreme? Commit now to true grace-driven holiness.

_____

_____

_____

_____

_____

_____

_____

_____

_____

_____

_____

_____

Action: Christian culture is full of examples of people who have missed the meaning of grace and the beauty of holiness. Read through a current Christian news publication or website. Look for examples of 1) a leader teaching behavior modification and/or works salvation, and 2) a leader compromising the truth of Scripture and excusing sin in the name of grace. What is the biblical balance that would restore both extremes to their true identity in Christ?

_____

_____

_____

_____

_____

_____

_____

_____

_____

_____

_____

_____

Journal: Meditate on Hebrews 12:1–2 and journal using the STAR method. What do you need to lay aside, and what do you need to take up in order to follow Christ?

Chapter Nine Notes

Abiding in Identity— at the Feet of Jesus

If you want to understand the topic of righteousness and set yourself on a clear path to abide in your identity in Christ, it is vital to understand the concept of abiding at His feet. So, in drawing this book to a close, I will begin by sharing three passages from my book *Abiding at the Feet of Jesus: A Study on the Beatitudes*—on abiding in Christ, the Beatitudes, and the essence of the Beatitudes.[40]

Abiding in Christ

I am the true vine, and My Father is the vinedresser. Every branch in Me that does not bear fruit He takes away; and every branch that bears fruit He prunes, that it may bear more fruit.

You are already clean because of the word which I have spoken to you. Abide in Me, and I in you. As the branch cannot bear fruit of itself, unless it abides in the vine, neither can you, unless you abide in Me. I am the vine, you are the branches. He who abides in Me, and I in him, bears much fruit; for without Me you can do nothing.

If anyone does not abide in Me, he is cast out as a branch and is withered; and they gather them and throw them into the fire, and they are burned. If you abide in Me, and My words abide in you, you will ask what you desire, and it shall be done for you. By this My Father is glorified, that you bear much fruit; so you will be My disciples.

As the Father loved Me, I also have loved you; abide in My love. If you keep My commandments, you will abide in My love, just as I have kept My Father's commandments and abide in His love. These things I have spoken to you, that My joy may remain in you, and that your joy may be full.

This is My commandment, that you love one another as I have loved you. Greater love has no one than this, than to lay down one's life for his friends. You are My friends if you do whatever I command you. No longer do I call you servants, for a servant does not know what his master is doing; but I have called you friends, for all things that I heard from My Father I have made known to you.

You did not choose Me, but I chose you and appointed you that you should go and bear fruit, and that your fruit should remain, that whatever you ask the Father in My name He may give you. These things I command you, that you love one another.

—John 15:1–17

To abide means to continue to remain connected. What better place to remain connected to Christ than sitting at His feet and learning from Him as He articulates the foundations of His kingdom? John 15 paints a beautiful picture of a life that is connected to the vine of Christ. This life produces Kingdom fruit that remains in the realm of eternity.

Some key thoughts about John 15:1–17:

- Note the intimacy between Christ and the Father.

- Note the intimacy that Christ wants with us, just like He has with the Father.

- Note the seriousness with which He speaks about bearing fruit and the consequences for those who do not.

- Note the total dependence on Him that we must have.

- Note how our prayer life changes when we abide in Him and have His heart.

- Note how the Father is glorified when we bear Kingdom fruit.

- Note the importance of love in this passage, how walking in His love is connected to our obeying His commands and loving others.

The Beatitudes, found in Matthew 5, are a blueprint that you can follow on your journey into a rich and meaningful intimacy with Christ that ultimately produces Kingdom fruit. Our study in the pages ahead focuses on some of the richest and most foundational words of Christ. These words, when applied, have the power to transform you and lead you into this intimate, abiding relationship. The goal of the Beatitudes is to pierce the heart of a religious, works-based, self-righteous culture and replace it with an intimate, abiding relationship with a living God.

The Beatitudes

And seeing the multitudes, [Jesus] went up on a mountain, and when He was seated His disciples came to Him. Then He opened His mouth and taught them, saying:

"Blessed are the poor in spirit, for theirs is the kingdom of heaven.

"Blessed are those who mourn, for they shall be comforted.

"Blessed are the meek, for they shall inherit the earth.

"Blessed are those who hunger and thirst for righteousness, for they shall be filled.

"Blessed are the merciful, for they shall obtain mercy.

"Blessed are the pure in heart, for they shall see God.

"Blessed are the peacemakers, for they shall be called sons of God.

"Blessed are those who are persecuted for righteousness' sake, for theirs is the kingdom of Heaven.

"Blessed are you when they revile and persecute you, and say all kinds of evil against you falsely for My sake. Rejoice and be exceedingly glad, for great is your reward in heaven, for so they persecuted the prophets who were before you."

—Matthew 5:1–12

The Latin word for blessed is *beatus*, from which we get the word *beatitude*.[41] In fact, each statement of Christ's begins with, "Blessed are." This statement is then followed up with two more statements. The first one describes *who* is blessed, and the second one explains *how* they are blessed. So, these Beatitudes are giving us

Kingdom insight into God's nature. If you want to be blessed, you must be the kind of person He describes in these important verses.

What do these seemingly contradictory statements mean to us today? Many of these Beatitudes do not seem to make sense. In fact, many of the statements seem to be paradoxical. What did Jesus mean when He said that the poor in spirit are blessed and that theirs is the Kingdom of Heaven? How could someone be blessed in the midst of mourning? Was Jesus speaking in vague, abstract terms? What did He want us to take away from this sermon?

A writer once said this about the Beatitudes: It's like someone went into the display window of life and switched all the price tags, and what we thought had value suddenly didn't. We will find statements like, "happy are the sad," or "satisfied are the hungry." None of it makes sense until you place yourself at the feet of Jesus on a mountainside over two thousand years ago.[42]

The Essence of the Beatitudes

Blessed are the poor in spirit: the essence of "poor in spirit" means that the Kingdom of Christ is for the repentant, spiritually bankrupt, dependent, and needy person. Material wealth has no bearing on this matter.

Blessed are those who mourn: The essence of biblical mourning is an act of reflection, cleansing, healing, and expression. It allows us to reflect the image of God out of a pure and redeemed heart.

Blessed are the meek: The essence of a biblically meek individual is someone who understands the God-given power that *ptochos* and *penthos* produce and who then submits to the authority of the Master.[43] This produces gentleness and peace, which brings life to those around the individual.

Blessed are those who hunger and thirst for righteousness: The essence of hungering for righteousness is having a sacred desire for identity in Christ alone. This hunger develops an intimacy with Christ that is the foundation of our faith.

Blessed are the merciful: The essence of mercy expresses the fact that when we receive the mercy of God, our natural response should be to extend mercy to others.

Blessed are the pure in heart: The essence of a pure heart is a heart that has been sifted and cleansed and has its affection fixed firmly on God.

Blessed are the peacemakers: The essence of a peacemaker is one who accepts the sacred responsibility to diffuse grace and truth into every situation and to offer the power of the Prince of Peace.

Blessed are those who are persecuted for righteousness' sake: The essence of the persecuted arises when the Spirit of God in you is at war with the spirit of the world in others.

The Beatitudes point the way into that intimate place with a pure and holy God. Religion keeps you on the outside, but these axioms with which Jesus began His ministry are drawing you into the heart of the Father. Isn't it amazing when you really look at the heart of the Beatitudes that they are a combination of who you are, what you do, and what happens to you? Taken all together, the Beatitudes encompass the fullness of your life.

When you abide in Christ, quick answers to your questions are no longer satisfying. You learn to become intimate with Christ, and He guides and directs your steps and satisfies your heart's desires. Many of the complicated topics are made clear through understanding and spiritual growth as you abide in Christ. In some cases, your questions may not receive an answer this side of heaven—instead they may require you to walk in faith, trusting God to be true to His Word.

This progression of living out the Beatitudes opens wide the doorway to an intimate, abiding relationship with Christ. As we truly embrace each of the Beatitudes, we will unlock the secrets of abiding in the Lord, and we will never be the same. Discipleship is not about arriving, but about abiding in Christ.

Then, Jesus said to those Jews who believed Him, "If you abide in My word, you are My disciples indeed."
—John 8:31

The model that Christ gave us for following Him is so simple that it confounds the wise of this world (1 Corinthians 1:27 KJV). Jesus told us to simply remain connected to Him. That's it. No ten-step programs or charts of accomplishment. Just stay connected to Him. Abide in Him.

God loves you with an everlasting love. He wants to intimately know you, and have you know Him, before He ever wants you to do anything for Him. He wants to be loved by you without condition. All of this only happens in an abiding relationship.

For a deeper look into the Beatitudes, be sure to read *Abiding at the Feet of Jesus: A Study on the Beatitudes.*

Experience, Grow, and Share

As you live out the Beatitudes in relationship with Jesus, remember also that abiding in your identity in Christ, while challenging, isn't complicated. Ultimately, living your identity in Christ is about three fundamental aspects: experiencing Christ, growing in Him, and sharing His love with others.

Abiding in Identity: Experience

As you learn to abide in your identity, you should find a way to experience Christ in every aspect of your day. This can happen in a time of prayer, worship, devotion, or a whole host of ways. It should not be limited to a timeframe set apart in your day. You should learn to experience Him all day, every day. To abide in Christ takes a big commitment. There are many things fighting for your time, and the tyranny of the urgent usually wins out. You must make Him the priority, including Him in every part of your day. Remember that Christ should be the center of your life instead of just at the top of a list for the day.

If I only spoke to my wife once a week, at church, our relationship would become strained over time. I would have stopped experiencing her. In the same way, many Christians think they can experience Christ once a week, in an hour-long church service, and expect to have a good relationship.

This limited amount of time together will slowly stress the relationship. You will quit abiding in Him and only go to Him on your terms when you want something. Your affections will be split between Him and many other things. You will quit hearing His leadings, and His blueprint will slowly fade away until you are living your life for you again.

This is a slippery slope that many Christians fall down. Unfortunately, many church leaders can sometimes feed this in church people. They like that they keep coming back to them as their source to reach God. This is dysfunctional and will not produce abiding believers or an abiding Church.

You must experience Christ for yourself and learn how to teach others to experience Christ for themselves.

Make your drive to work a time of abiding. Acknowledge Christ in your work and make your work worship to Him. Washing dishes can be a time of worship and communion with Him. Folding laundry can be surrounded by the presence of God. Are you getting it now? Make it a commitment to experience Him all day, every day.

And this is eternal life, that they may know You, the only true God, and Jesus Christ whom You have sent.
—John 17:3

...that I may know Him and the power of His resurrection, and the fellowship of His sufferings, being conformed to His death...

—Philippians 3:10

Abiding in Identity: Grow

This part of the process involves growing in your fellowship with Christ. This is where people grow in righteousness. Grow in your perception of who God is and who you are in relationship with Him. Grow in the gifts that God has given you. Grow in fellowship with Him. Grow in your understanding of His grace and love toward you. Grow in the knowledge of the Word. Grow in your faith.

Every day, you should find practical ways to develop in your relationship with God. This could involve a daily Bible study, a church discipleship class, leading your family in devotions, or many other things. The more you can learn about God and the Bible, the more He can grow you and lead you, according to His will. This has to happen alongside experiencing Him.

You don't want to gain knowledge without relationship. However, when the two work hand in hand, you will see God reveal new things to you. The Bible tells us that "knowledge puffs up, but love edifies" (1 Corinthians 8:1). If you have knowledge only, it does not produce what God intended in your life.

Many believers experience Christ and let Him be their Savior, providing an escape from hell. Then they stop there and don't pursue allowing God to be their Lord.

When Christ is your Lord, you are growing every day in personal abandonment and absolute trust in Him. You experience eternal life, here and now, not just in heaven.

This part of the process needs to involve commitment and participation in a local abiding church. You need a safe place to be discipled. Many times, I come across people who just need to sit in a season of healing, restoration, and growing. They need a safe place to mend, and an abiding church should be just that.

Instead, many times, these people try to get out what is on the inside, so they can deal with their pain, and the atmosphere they are in ridicules and condemns them. An abiding church offers a "grow" portion of ministry that celebrates authenticity and transparency. This will be a huge part of people growing in Christ. Find a local church that you can be accountable to in order to help you grow in your identity in Christ.

> But grow in grace, and in the knowledge of our Lord and Savior Jesus Christ. To him be glory, both now and forever. Amen.
> —2 Peter 3:18

> But, as it is written: Eye has not seen, nor ear heard, Nor have entered into the heart of man, The things which God has prepared for those who love Him. But God has revealed them to us, through His Spirit. For the Spirit searches all things, yes, the deep things of God.
> —1 Corinthians 2:9–10

Abiding in Identity: Share

This part of the process involves sharing the love of Christ in practical ways. When you experience and grow in God every day, sharing Him will be a natural outflow of your life. You will find ways to share His love with people in your area of influence.

There are people whom God has placed in your life who may never hear the message of Christ outside of you sharing it with them. This is a responsibility and a privilege. Remember that your life is about bringing glory to God. What better way to bring Him glory than to share your story of how His love transformed your life and that He can do the same for others?

God will give you divine appointments with people and open doors to simply talk about Him. You can use this process to share His love. It's less about scriptures and theology and more about letting them know that God loves them and wants to be in a relationship with them.

I want to warn you, though, that sharing the love of Christ becomes addicting. When you share His love, and someone comes to know Him, it is the most awesome experience on earth. Heaven rejoices, and you get more excited to share Him with even more people. I have had many people, over the years, come alive when they learn this simple vision and process. They are amazed that they understand their relationship with God so much clearer. They have a simplified, daily focus that keeps them in proximity to Christ and not just doing things for Him. Many have said that they share their faith regularly because they understand this and have become alive in Christ. Sharing is easy when you use Christ's method.

Ask God to teach you how to abide in Him. Ask Him to show you areas in your life that need to be cut off and removed so that fruit can grow. Give God permission to discipline and prune that which will make you grow. If you can walk in this biblical fellowship, then you can introduce this abiding-in-Christ identity to others.

Teaching transformation is slow and tough as it takes time for people to go through this process and start to see the results on the outside. The key is that it is true and lasting fruit because the inner issue was addressed and made right.

Most religions stress us doing something to be in their god's good graces. They have us pursuing a god to be good enough for him. Christianity is God's story of Him pursuing us. He says: "I understand your sin and failure, and yet I have provided a way to be in relationship with you."

Unfortunately, many see the Christian church as another system of dos and don'ts that expresses what we are against, rather than what we are for. Remember, the church is the hope of the world, and Christ is the answer to our world's sin problem. We must examine our lives in light of this. As an abider in Christ, it is vital in your sharing Christ to allow this abiding principle of transformation to permeate the DNA of how you do this. You will see fruit like never before that is sustainable and reproducible. What is more compelling than eternal fruit?

A person who has an abiding relationship with Jesus has been, and will continue to be, transformed. This person understands their relationship with God and has allowed that to change his heart. He does not pursue a lifestyle of sin, because he has found the greater joy of being transformed into the image of God.

This transformation has removed many of the sinful tendencies from his heart and made his heart to honor Christ. He views his struggles with sin as an opportunity to sit with Jesus and allow His power and love to conquer that sin nature.

The more time this one spends with Jesus, the more he reflects His love and heart. That, my friend, is a disciple of Christ. If you want to fully experience and abide in your identity in Christ, then all you must do is learn to abide in Him. Give it a try. You will never be the same.

WORKBOOK

Conclusion Questions

Question: How can you experience Christ on a daily basis?

_____

_____

_____

_____

_____

_____

_____

_____

_____

_____

_____

Question: In what areas are you growing and becoming more like Christ? Where is growth needed?

_____

_____

_____

_____

_____

_____

_____

_____

_____

_____

_____

Action: Whom has God placed on your heart that needs Him? How will seeing an abiding relationship draw them to Christ in a way that religion never could? Plan a time and a way to share the joy of your abiding relationship with Christ with this person.

_____

_____

_____

_____

_____

_____

_____

_____

_____

_____

_____

_____

Journal: Memorize and meditate on Matthew 5:1–12. Go through the STAR journal process with this passage. Purpose to make abiding in Christ the essence of your life and identity.

APPENDIX A

Journaling 101 by Rocky Fleming

On your journey to intimacy with Christ, one thing that can greatly assist you is journaling. This is a foreign concept to most people. However, journaling can be a gift from God to you. Many times, we learn to internalize our thoughts, keeping them hidden in the deep recesses of our minds. Journaling is a way to help you get those issues out of your heart and onto the altar before God.

In this technological age of high-speed communication, written words have been lost. Today, most of our thoughts and reflections about life—if they even make it out of our heads—are condensed into brief digital formats, which are then deleted in cyberspace before they have a chance to sink into our consciousness. There is power in the written word on paper. God wants us to slow down, be still for a few moments with Him, and just like He instructed countless people from Moses to Paul, He wants us to write down the revelations He gives us.

In the pages of this book, there is a lot of information for you to prayerfully navigate. We have included this simple form of journaling to help you put down on paper some key things that may be speaking the loudest to you.

When you write things down there is a tendency to remember more and create further action steps to implement the learning pieces. If you are going to invest the time to read this book, it would greatly benefit you to utilize journaling through the workbook section at the end of each chapter. If you are inspired to become an abiding leader of an abiding church, there will be much to process, and this method can help you to simplify this.

STAR Journaling Exercise Template

#1 Scripture Read/Promise Given/Question Asked

Read the verse and/or question and walk through the STAR/SPAR process. Pause and prayerfully meditate on what is being said, read, or asked.

#2 Thought Conveyed/Promise Given

In this part, write down what this means to you so that you can clearly understand the question, scripture, thought, or promise. Make it personal to get the most out of it.

#3 Application Made

How does this teaching apply to me right now? How does this apply to my leadership context?

#4 Response Given

What can I do to immediately to apply this to my life? How should I respond/react to this promise or instruction? What are some long-term things I need to respond to?

Used with permission from Rocky Fleming and www.Influencers.org.[44]

Further Resources

The Journey is a nine- to twelve-month process, with most groups meeting every other week. It is divided into three main segments, called Enlightened, Enabled, and Expressing.

The Enlightened segment of the Journey is the foundation of the process. The step-by-step understanding of the four personal aspects of God (He Knows, He Cares, He Is Willing, and He Is Able) is designed to help the participant realize that God is a loving, caring, and intimate God who wants to involve Himself in every area of the participant's life. This new understanding should guide the participant to the goal of being willing to trust God with his life and prepares the way for the second segment of the Journey.

The Enabled segment of the Journey focuses on an abiding, intimate relationship with Jesus. This segment helps the participant understand how the Holy Spirit "enables" him to develop this new level of intimacy. He is guided through an understanding of the "fruit of the Spirit" and how this fruit enables the use of the "gifts of the Spirit." This should help him to better understand his role and purpose in the work of God's kingdom. Above all else, the Enabled segment should guide the participant toward the goal of releasing control of his life and experiencing the joy of personal abandonment found in his abiding relationship with Jesus.

The Expressing segment of the Journey is the culmination of the Journey process. The principles of "Being a God Seeker," "Being a God Abider," and "Live It Out" are used as the guide to help the participant fully understand the entire Journey. He is introduced to the concept of servant leadership within his marriage, his family, and the world around him. He is challenged to grasp the concept of "blooming where he is planted" and how he is now ready to partner with God to influence his world in a supernatural way. At the end of the Journey, the participant is released to take the name "Influencer" and begin to bear fruit that lasts by expressing Christlike love to all those around him.

The Journey experience has three main components for each participant.

The first is his personal "treasure hunt," conducted during the days between sessions. This is the core of the Journey and the place where heart transformation takes place. This "treasure hunt" guides the participant toward the "Inner Chamber," where intimacy with Christ is discovered and experienced.

The second component is the one-on-one time between the guide and the participant. This individual time is critical to the participant's journey as the guide and the participant share their life stories.

The third component is the group sessions, designed for the group to discuss their journey and share discovered truth. Each session enhances the other two components and ties the Journey together.

This Journey process will lay a strong foundation that you can build upon as you pursue your long-term growth track.

Influencers is a ministry with the goal of guiding people into an intimate, abiding relationship with Jesus Christ. They accomplish this through Journey groups, who journey together for nine months, each desiring a closer proximity to the Father. Participants discover God in a most personal way through Scripture, journaling, group discussion, prayer, and study materials.

Jesus said, "I am the vine; you are the branches. If you remain in me and I in you, you will bear much fruit; apart from me you can do nothing" (John 15:5 NIV). For years, good Christian people have been striving to bear fruit for God. However, they have missed the part about "remaining in Him." Influencers helps people press the pause button in life, so that they can take time to seek Jesus and find renewed hope and purpose.

Thousands of people—and increasingly, women and married couples as well—have gone on this Journey worldwide, and thousands more are finding their way to this life-giving process. If you would like to know more about Influencers and the Journey and how to start a group in your city, go to the website at www.influencers.org.

Other Resources

- *I'm a Catalyst* membership manual by Catalyst

Church

- *The Abiding Church: Creating, Cultivating, and Stewarding a Culture of Discipleship* by Nate Sweeney
- *Abiding at the Feet of Jesus: A Study on the Beatitudes* by Nate Sweeney
- *Journey to the Inner Chamber* by Rocky Fleming
- *Knowing Christ and Making Him Known* by Nate Sweeney
- *5-2-1 Leadership Planning*

REFERENCES

Notes

1. Carson, D. A. *Love in Hard Places.* Crossway, 2002, p. 61.

2. Brown, Michael. Facebook post. May 14, 2017. https://www.facebook.com/AskDr-Brown/posts/1947488478610078.

3. Fleming, Rocky. "Journaling." *Influencers Global Ministries.* www.influencers.org/journaling.

4. Luther, Martin. "The Freedom of a Christian." 1520. In "Martin Luther: On the Freedom of a Christian," Internet Modern History Sourcebook, *Fordham University.* https://sourcebooks.fordham.edu/mod/luther-freedomchristian.asp.

5. Ravenhill, Leonard. *Why Revival Tarries.* Bethany House, 2004, p. 71.

6. Bennett, Sanford Fillmore. "In the Sweet By and By." 1868. In *Hymanry.org.* https://hymnary.org/text/theres_a_land_that_is_fairer_than_day_an.

7. Lloyd-Jones, David Martyn. *Studies in the Sermon on the Mount.* Eerdmans, 1961, p. 244.

8. Taylor, Jeremy. *The Whole Works of Rt. Rev. Jeremy Taylor.* Vol. 1. Frederick Westley and A. H. Davis, 1836, p. 399.

9. Meyers, Jeremy. "Is Crusade Evangelism Effective?" *Redeeming God.* https://redeeminggod.com/crusade-evangelism-effective.

10. Carson, D. A. *The God Who Is There: Finding Your Place in God's Story.* Baker Books, 2010, p. 173.

11. Willard, Dallas. *The Great Omission: Reclaiming Jesus's Essential Teachings on Discipleship.* Harper One, 2009.

12. "Strong's G1849 – exousia." *Blue Letter Bible.* https://www.blueletterbible.org/lang/lexicon/lexicon.cfm?Strongs=G1849&t=KJV.

13. Warren, Rick. *The Purpose Driven Life.* Zondervan, 2002.

14. Wenner, Emma. "July Religion Bestsellers: 'Purpose Driven Life' Makes a Comeback; James Patterson Tops." *Publishers Weekly.* August 9, 2017. https://www.publishersweekly.com/pw/by-topic/industry-news/religion/article/74435-july-religion-bestsellers-purpose-driven-life-makes-a-comeback-james-patterson-tops.html.

15. Cammaerts, Emile. *The Laughing Prophet: The Seven Virtues and G. K. Chesterton.* 2nd ed. Methuen, 1937, p. 211.

16. Johnson, Bill. Facebook post. April 17, 2014. https://www.facebook.com/BillJohnsonMinistries/posts/10152196064053387.

17. "Strong's G1343 – dikaiosynē." *Blue Letter Bible.* https://www.blueletterbible.org/lang/lexicon/lexicon.cfm?Strongs=G1343&t=KJV.

18. Nate Sweeney. *Abiding at the Feet of Jesus: A Study on the Beatitudes.* Sermon To Book, 2018. This chapter is an excerpt from my book *Abiding at the Feet of Jesus: A Study on the Beatitudes.* I have decided to include it in this book as well because it lays a foundation regarding the triune nature and lays to rest many questions that might otherwise arise.

19. Lewis, C. S. "The Weight of Glory." *Theology* 43, no. 257 (November 1, 1941), p. 263–274.

20. "Strong's G1467 – egkrateuomai." *Blue Letter Bible.* https://www.blueletterbible.org/lang/lexicon/lexicon.cfm?Strongs=G1467&t=KJV.

21. "Strong's G145 – aisthētērion." *Blue Letter Bible.* https://www.blueletterbible.org/lang/lexicon/lexicon.cfm?Strongs=G145&t=KJV.

22. "Strong's G3713 – orgē." *Blue Letter Bible.* https://www.blueletterbible.org/lang/lexicon/lexicon.cfm?Strongs=G3709&t=KJV.

23. "Strong's G3709 – oregō." *Blue Letter Bible.* https://www.blueletterbible.org/lang/lexicon/lexicon.cfm?strongs=G3713&t=KJV.

24. "Strong's G4413 – prōtos." *Blue Letter Bible.* https://www.blueletterbible.org/lang/lexicon/ lexicon.cfm?Strongs=G4413&t=KJV.

25. Luther, "The Freedom of a Christian."

26. "Prodigal." *Dictionary.com.* http://www.dictionary.com/browse/prodigal?s=t.

27. Rosemond, John. "Postmodern Psychological Parenting." In *Parenting by the Book: Biblical Wisdom for Raising Your Child.* Simon and Schuster, 2007, p. 31–69.

28. Adler, Jerry. "Freud in Our Midst." March 26, 2006. *Newsweek.* http://www.newsweek.com/freud-our-midst-106495.

29. Rohr, Richard. *Adam's Return: The Five Promises of Male Initiation.* Crossroad, 2004, p. 8, 101–103, 173.

30. Butterfield, Rosaria. "Love Your Neighbor Enough to Speak the Truth: A Response to Jen Hatmaker." October 31, 2016. *The Gospel Coalition.* https://www.thegospelcoalition.org/article/love-your-neighbor-enough-to-speak-truth.

31. Bonhoeffer, Dietrich. *The Cost of Discipleship.* Collier Books, 1963, p. 99.

32. "Abandon." *American Heritage Dictionary of the English Language.* 5th edition. 2016. Quoted in *The Free Dictionary.* https://www.thefreedictionary.com /abandonments.

33. Driscoll, Mark. *A Call to Resurgence: Will Christianity Have a Funeral or a Future?* Tyndale, 2013, p. 11–12.

34. "2018 World Watch List." January 10, 2018. *Open Doors International.* https://opendoorsinternational. exposure.co/2018-world-watch-list-top-10.

35. Spurgeon, Charles. "The Monster Dragged to Light." In *Sermons.* 10th series. R. Carter, 1883, p. 133.

36. Hovey, E. Paul. In *The Westminster Collection of Christian Quotations.* Edited by Martin H. Manser. Westminster John Knox Press, 2001, p. 11.

37. Pink, A. W. "Part 1: Signs of the Times." *Studies on Saving Faith.* Reiner Publications, 1976, p. 11.

38. Crowley, Aleister. *Liber AL vel Legis.* Tunis, 1925.

39. "Strong's H7495 – rapha'." *Blue Letter Bible.* https://www.blueletterbible.org/lang/lexicon/lexicon.cfm?Strongs=H7495&t=KJV.

40. Sweeney, Nate. *Abiding at the Feet of Jesus: A Study on the Beatitudes.* Sermon To Book, 2018.

41. "Beatitude." *Oxford English Living Dictionaries.* Oxford University Press. https://en.oxford dictionaries.com/definition/beatitude.

42. MacArthur, John. *The MacArthur New Testament Commentary.* Moody, 2011.

43. "Strong's G4434 – ptōchos." *Blue Letter Bible.* https://www.blueletterbible.org/lang/lexicon/lexicon.cfm?Strongs=G4434&t=KJV.

"Strong's G3997 – penthos." *Blue Letter Bible.* https://www.blueletterbible.org/lang/lexicon/lexicon.cfm?t=kjv&strongs=g3997.

44. Fleming, "Journaling."

About the Author

Nate Sweeney would be considered an average person, someone who loves his family, community, and church. The major factor that sets him apart is his passion to Know Christ and Make Him Known. This vision is at the forefront of Nate's daily focus and drives him to stay connected to Christ and share that relationship with others. Nate pursues this vision in his home with his wife, Monica, and their three kids.

Nate has served in many ministry capacities since he graduated from Bible school in 1997. He is the directional leader of Catalyst Church in Bentonville, Arkansas. Nate is the founder and directional leader of The Abiding Network, and he sits on the Influencers Ministry global board as a church relations leader.

Nate speaks with experience, as he has led his church to be transformed into an Abiding Church, and his role has become supported by the great leaders who have been raised up in this church. At the time of this publishing, Nate has mentored, coached, and helped disciple hundreds of church leaders nationally.

It is evident, through Nate's ministry, that people are challenged to daily experience God and grow in their relationship with Him, while discovering what He has called them to do in life and share His love in practical ways.

About Sermon To Book

SermonToBook.com began with a simple belief: that sermons should be touching lives, *not* collecting dust. That's why we turn sermons into high-quality books that are accessible to people all over the globe.

Turning your sermon series into a book exposes more people to God's Word, better equips you for counseling, accelerates future sermon prep, adds credibility to your ministry, and even helps make ends meet during tight times.

John 21:25 tells us that the world itself couldn't contain the books that would be written about the work of Jesus Christ. Our mission is to try anyway. Because in heaven, there will no longer be a need for sermons or books. Our time is now.

If God so leads you, we'd love to work with you on your sermon or sermon series.

Visit www.sermontobook.com to learn more.

Made in the USA
Columbia, SC
28 March 2019